Scotland
by Rail

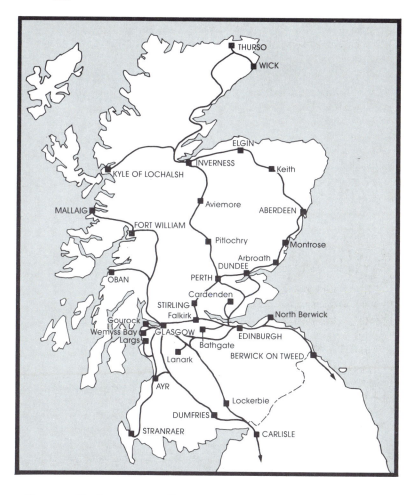

THURSO

WICK

ELGIN

INVERNESS

KYLE OF LOCHALSH

Keith

MALLAIG

Aviemore

ABERDEEN

FORT WILLIAM

Pitlochry

Montrose

Arbroath
DUNDEE

OBAN

PERTH

Cardenden

STIRLING

Falkirk

North Berwick

Gourock
Wemyss Bay
Largs

GLASGOW

EDINBURGH

Bathgate

BERWICK ON TWEED

Lanark

AYR

Lockerbie

DUMFRIES

STRANRAER

CARLISLE

A guide to the routes,
scenery and towns

ABOUT THIS BOOK

Scotland by Rail is one of a series of guidebooks being compiled by the Railway Development Society – an independent voluntary organisation of rail-users who are campaigning for the improvement and greater usage of rail transport.

Every editor relies on the knowledge and expertise of others and I am grateful to all the various authors who have contributed so willingly to the success of this book.

All the information contained in the articles was correct at the time of writing, but circumstances can change and readers are advised to check locally details of such matters as train frequencies and admission times.

This book, in common with other titles in the series, has been written with the general reader in mind, so railway technical terms have been kept to a minimum. An 'up' line or platform is used by trains to London or another principal city, whereas a 'down' line or platform is the opposite. A DMU is a diesel multiple-unit or railcar, as against a locomotive-hauled train.

Finally, I am indebted to Trevor Garrod and John Lark for their editorial and research assistance; to Peter Wakefield and Anthony Kay for maps; to Steven Binks for line diagrams; and to Hugh Neville, Secretary to RDS (Scotland), for his help and suggestions.

Brian Chaplin.

Front cover: County March summit, Tyndrum. (*Photo:* Chris Burton)
Back cover: Forth rail bridge from North Queensferry. (*Photo:* Gordon C. Henderson)
Inside front cover: Stirling Castle. (*Photo:* N. Jinkerson)
Inside back cover: Oban at night. (*Photo:* C. J. Nicholas)

CONTENTS

INTRODUCTION

The other volumes in this series have covered various parts of England and Wales – some small and some rather larger. The present volume seeks to provide a foretaste of an entire country whose railways cover some 1,500 miles.

These lines include busy Inter-City routes, an electrified suburban system and single tracks that penetrate some of the loneliest and most unspoilt parts of the United Kingdom. In this book, we could not cover every mile, but we have succeeded in covering by far the greater part of the network and, we hope, have demonstrated its value to resident and visitor alike.

Scotland has a different feel to it. It has a different identity to England, and this includes aspects of culture, tradition, and history as well as differences in the legal system and even diet! So it is very well worth a visit, and how better than by train – although one may need to use the bus or even the ferry to fill in some of the parts of the country not served by rail. Lots of visitors rush to the Highlands and Edinburgh (perhaps at Festival time) and do not find their way to other places. The Railway Development Society (Scotland) urges you to discover the rest!

Within Scotland we always find variety. The north-east really is different from the south-west. The scenery, architecture, and agriculture reflect richness and often grandeur. Some non-Scots, especially, may wonder how best to appreciate this variety, and a suggested itinerary may be of interest to them.

Enter Scotland via the East Coast route from London King's Cross, and travel to Edinburgh. If time permits have an excursion, sadly now only possible by bus, to the delightful Borders towns of Selkirk, Hawick, or Melrose. From Edinburgh, take the train via the world-famous Forth and Tay Bridges to Dundee, and thence along the coast further to Aberdeen. Throughout, this route is fascinating, especially as it passes near small villages, rocky coves, sandy bays, and over the majestic bridges themselves.

From the Granite City of Aberdeen we go to Inverness, possibly via a few distilleries, and from the Highland capital of Inverness we head north to Wick and Thurso or over the spectacular route to Kyle of Lochalsh. A ferry then makes a delightful journey down to Mallaig, when we can travel by the scenic West Highland line to Glasgow. Alternatively, we can return to Inverness and take the dramatic Highland line down to historic Perth and Stirling and thence to Glasgow.

After a look round Scotland's largest city and the Clyde coast we could return south via the West Coast line and Lockerbie to Carlisle and London Euston; or, if time allowed, take a diversion via the newly electrified route to Ayr, thence over the scenic uplands to Stranraer, returning to Dumfries (sadly by bus) then train to Carlisle. If time allowed, extra excursions could be made, especially out from Glasgow to the coast or Loch Lomond.

This guide will help you to get the most out of your travels round Scotland, especially if you are interested in scenery, wildlife, walking, cycling, history, archaeology, sport, shopping, or entertainment. In other words, Scotland offers everything.

A final point, also worth bearing in mind – during summer Scotland has more daylight hours than places further south – so you have more time in which to see it!

BERWICK UPON TWEED–EDINBURGH

By Norman Renton

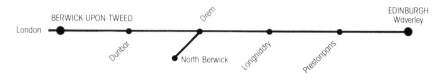

Edinburgh is served by Inter-City 125 diesel trains from London King's Cross, via York and Newcastle – with the fastest train, 'The Flying Scotsman', covering the 393 miles in four hours and thirty-five minutes. Masts and wires are now going up along the route, and from 1991 electric expresses will be linking the capitals of England and Scotland.

This route to the north, called the 'East Coast Main Line' by British Rail, is described in the English companion volumes to *Scotland by Rail*, and we shall take up the story as it approaches the Border, running close to the breezy Northumberland coast.

Shortly before arrival at Berwick Upon Tweed we cross the Royal Border Bridge with its spectacular twenty-eight-arch span from where we enjoy beautiful views of the town and the Tweed Estuary. This ancient Border town's medieval history saw it change hands between Scotland and England many times.

Soon after leaving Berwick, at the start of our 57-mile journey to Edinburgh, the border between England and Scotland is clearly defined by a large trackside sign which can be seen from the train. Then follows a wonderfully scenic stretch with the railway hugging the cliffs above the North Sea for 5 miles to the fishing village of Burnmouth.

We leave the coast now and travel some miles inland through the rich agricultural merse of Berwickshire to the small market town of Duns. Continuing northwards, we commence the gradual ascent along the valley of the Eye to Granthouse. A mile or two on we come to the detour round the ill-fated Penmanshiel Tunnel where, in March 1979, two men tragically lost their lives. The tunnel collapsed during excavation work to lower the tracks to accommodate larger Freightliner trains. The same tunnel had been in the news in August 1948 when torrential summer rains caused flooding problems on the East Coast Main Line.

The train soon passes the small village of Cockburnspath and again runs for 5 miles along the coast, past the soon-to-be-commissioned Torness nuclear power station, to the historically famous and popular resort of Dunbar. This is the only stop on the East Coast Main Line between Berwick and Edinburgh, the other stations having succumbed to the infamous Beeching axe in the 1960s. Three centuries ago Dunbar was an important fishing port, but now the harbour is quieter with only a small fishing fleet. Eighty feet above the entrance to the harbour are the ruins of Dunbar Castle, built to defend the gateway to the eastern plains. The John Muir Country Park has a golf-course, picnic sites, fine beaches, and a cliff-top nature trail.

Proceeding west from Dunbar, we pass through the pretty village of East Linton and on through rich farming country to the hamlet of Drem. This is the junction for the branch line that runs north-eastwards for 4½ miles to North Berwick. Let us leave the East Coast Main Line for a moment and take a trip to this attractive seaside resort. Unfortunately, however, main-line trains no longer stop at Drem, so we must commence the thirty-five-minute journey to North Berwick at Edinburgh Waverley.

The Edinburgh–North Berwick service uses the East Coast Main Line for 18 miles, calling at Prestonpans, Longniddry, and Drem. Leaving Drem, we proceed along the single track (which is in effect an extended siding) through a deep rock cutting past the now-closed small station of Dirleton, a lovely village more than a mile from its station. Shortly we hear the brakes being applied, for, despite being still ¾ mile from the terminus, we have begun a fairly steep descent in a cutting and so must approach the station with great caution. Two years ago the antiquated Victorian station was demolished, and the line truncated by 200 yards to make way for a car park, leaving a basic platform and waiting shelter.

It is interesting to note that in 1968 the British Railways Board published closure proposals for the North Berwick line; but after concerted efforts by the local MP, the Town Council, many commuters, and other bodies, the then Transport Minister granted a reprieve. However, from January 1970 the service was restricted to two morning and two evening commuter trains daily with additional trains on Saturdays; but over the years British Rail have added extra trains and now provide an excellent two-hourly service throughout the day with additional trains at peak times. The ageing DMUs with which it is currently operated are to be replaced in 1987 with new Sprinters.

A short walk down the hill from the station takes us to North Berwick's main street,

North Berwick. (*Photo:* J. Brooks)

which has a mixture of good quality shops and the usual high street stores serving a population of approximately 5,000. The town is flanked to the east and west by two bays divided by a rocky headland where we find the busy, red sandstone harbour, which offers sanctuary to a fleet of boats and the popular outdoor swimming-pool. There are fine sands, an interesting shoreline of rocks for the children, and magnificent seaward views over the Forth Estuary to Fife and various islands, the largest being the famous 350-foot-high Bass Rock. This is a well-known nesting place for thousands of gannets and many other seabirds, and during the summer months motor boats sail to it from the harbour. Golfers will find two very challenging courses, and for the less energetic there are two putting-courses as well as many interesting walks. In all, a resort well worth a visit, with accommodation to suit all tastes; the Tourist Information Office is at 18 Quality Street (telephone 2197).

Returning to the East Coast Main Line towards Edinburgh, we soon pass through the former village and now fairly large dormitory town of Longniddry from where trains once travelled to the East Lothian county town of Haddington. Glimpses of the Forth can be seen on the way to Prestonpans, scene of the famous battle fought in 1745 between Bonnie Prince Charlie and General Cope, and later a town with such industries as pottery, brewing, and coal-mining. After skirting Musselburgh and Portobellow, we finally reach Edinburgh, Scotland's capital city and our journey's end.

CITY OF EDINBURGH
by Arthur Bennett and Trevor Garrod

Scotland's capital city boasts one of the finest Neo-classical town-planning developments in Britain, besides a compact medieval town with a single street, The Royal Mile, from the Royal Holyrood Palace to the east, to the towering Castle in the west. The city's Waverley Station is claimed to be the second largest in Britain, and lies inconspicuously in a hollow below the Old Town, where it is approached on foot by the apparently endless Waverley Steps, and two short service roads to reveal a spacious concourse and platforms. There is direct access to the palatial North British Hotel marking the east end of the principal thoroughfare, Princes Street.

'Waverley' brings to mind the novels of Sir Walter Scott, and his ornate memorial immediately catches the eye when one is leaving the station and looking west across Princes Street Gardens, towards the two galleries and the Caledonian Hotel beyond. To the left is the extensive Castle dominating the skyline and on the right the handsome buildings of Princes Street. A loch was drained to form the gardens and to separate the New Town from the Old, and the railway had to be concealed in a deep cutting to preserve the amenities.

A walk of about ¾ mile along Princes Street, with fine views of the Castle, brings one to Lothian Road and the site of the terminus of the defunct Caledonian Railway, of which the pink-stone hotel is the survivor. Turn left and left again up Johnson Terrace and you reach the castle, containing, among other things the Scottish United Services Museum. From the battlements enjoy the wide views across the city, the Forth and the hills in Fife, and admire the great cannon *Mons Meg*: an A4 steam locomotive of the same name used to rumble along the railway below.

Leave the Castle and walk down through the Lawn Market and High Street where every building is of some interest, and visit St Giles' Cathedral on your way to Holyrood Palace at the end of the Royal Mile and situated in a large park under the shadow of an extinct volcano named Arthur's Seat.

Alternatively you may turn left off the High Street, return to Princes Street and turn right into St Andrew's Square, a part of the New Town, with a 50-metre-high monument in the middle of a formal garden, and a few distinguished buildings from the eighteenth century. Proceed along George Street to its termination in Charlotte Square, designed by Robert Adam, and view the extensive terraces and crescents of the New Town, housing some 14,000 people, and make more attractive the slope down towards the Water of Leith. Turn left in Charlotte Square and return to the station along Princes Street.

If you wish to learn more about 'The Athens of the North', the Tourist Information Centre at 5 Waverley Bridge (telephone 226 6591) within a few yards of the station will provide numerous maps and guidebooks. Most of the exploration of Edinburgh will be by foot or vehicle, since the once-extensive suburban railway system was abandoned in the 1960s, but sufficient remains to provide a route on the south of the city, and a feasibility study for this is in progress. A more ambitious scheme to provide a comprehensive metro system throughout the city has been presented to the Regional Council, but must await a change in the political climate before being discussed.

CARLISLE–CARSTAIRS–MOTHERWELL–GLASGOW

by Andrew N. Stephen

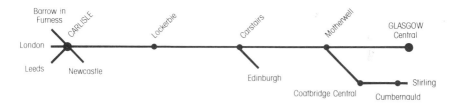

As you head north from Carlisle's Citadel Station, Scotland is but a few minutes away. Your train makes spirited headway across the flat land at the mouths of the Eden and Esk rivers. To the west can be seen the vast expanse of the Solway Firth as the train crosses the Esk. To the west can be seen a low viaduct. The other main west coast artery to Scotland, the A74 dual carriageway, crosses overhead. A few miles to the east is the site of the Battle of Solway Moss (1542) and the Ministry of Defence depot at Longtown.

Sharp-eyed travellers may just catch a glimpse of the 'Welcome to Scotland' signs as the train crosses the small River Sark to enter the Kingdom of Caledonia. The line on which you are travelling was once part of the Caledonian Railway. To the left, the route to Glasgow via Dumfries, the old Glasgow & South Western, curves away. Traffic to Stranraer *en route* to Northern Ireland also travels on this line.

Skirting the village of Gretna, famous for its marrying runaway couples, we also pass the scene of the most horrific disaster in British railway history, when, at Quintinshill on 22 May 1915, a laden troop train and two others met their end.

The villages of Kirkpatrick Fleming, Kirtlebridge, and Ecclefechan rush by as we head for the market town of Lockerbie. Most trains, however, bypass this sole remaining station on the route between Carlisle and Carstairs.

Climbing farther into the Southern Uplands, we soon pass through the village of Beattock, from whence a branch line once served the nearby tourist town of Moffat, and a few miles farther north approach the boundary between Dumfries and Galloway and Strathclyde Regions – at a point where the A74 passes below. Squeezing through the rolling hills, we pass close to the source of the River Clyde at Clyde Law (1,790 feet) and soon attain Beattock Summit, named after the settlement.

Now that the hard climb is over, the train hurries through the village of Elvanfoot. It was from this remote spot that a branch line once climbed high into the Lowther Hills through Leadhills to Wanlockhead, the highest village in Scotland. This branch, opened in 1902, was the highest in the land, attaining 1,498 feet, until its demise in 1939. However, an ambitious project to restore part of this railway, albeit as a narrow-gauge line, is currently being undertaken by the Lowthers Railway Society.

Sweeping onwards, the train curves past the village of Crawford and we cross the infant River Clyde for the first time. Through Abington, where the A74 parts company with the railway line, we follow the river onwards through Symington and Thankerton, viewing to the west the conical hill of Tinto (2,320 feet). Soon we are approaching Carstairs Junction, where some trains divide to allow a portion to serve Edinburgh.

The old county town of Lanark is on a hill to the west a few miles north of Carstairs, and a possible glimpse of an orange-liveried train shows that we are now in the area served by the extensive Strathclyde surburban rail network. The abundance of glasshouses denotes the extensive market gardening of 'Scotch' tomatoes in this area. A mile from Lanark is the village of New Lanark, founded in 1784 by the philanthropist David Dale, whose son-in-law, the reformer Robert Owen, instituted many welfare schemes for the workers in the village's cotton-spinning factories. The entire village is in the process of being preserved as it was in Owen's day and is well worth a visit. (Travel by the SPTE local train to Lanark.)

Carluke and Wishaw are passed as the train rapidly approaches the outskirts of Motherwell, whose Ravenscraig and Dalziel (pronounced Dee-yell) works of British Steel dominate the town. Interestingly, the metal for the great Cunard ships *Queen Mary* and *Queen Elizabeth* was forged here. The name Motherwell derives from 'Modyrwaile' (the well, or pool, of the Virgin Mary), the site of which is marked by a plaque in Ladywell Road, Wishaw (originally Waygateshaw). During the past thirty years, Motherwell's superb swimming-pool has been the training centre for three world record-holders and many British record-holders.

Soon after leaving Motherwell's busy station, the main line northwards to Stirling and Perth (described below) branches away to the right, while to the left are the works of the Motherwell Bridge Company. The fast, direct line from Motherwell to Glasgow bypasses Hamilton to the west and Bellshill to the east, both served by suburban trains on the Hamilton Circle service. Shortly before the M74 overbridge at Uddingston can be seen the works of the Blue Circle Cement Company. The now much larger River Clyde is crossed, yet again, on a high bridge soon after Uddingston.

Through Newton and Cambuslang, the train heads towards the Royal Burgh of Rutherglen, named after its founder King Reuther (c. 200 BC), which received its Royal Charter from David I in 1126 and for fifty years included the then much smaller Glasgow within its boundaries. However, since the last decade's reform of local government, the tables have been turned and the town now forms part of the southern approaches to Glasgow. The city of Glasgow looms before us as a slowing of the train for a right-handed curve towards yet another, and final, crossing of the Clyde leads directly into ScotRail's spacious and modernised Central Station – right in the heart of this warm and friendly city.

The abundance of fine hotels, restaurants, museums, cinemas, theatres, and shops, as well as the numerous parks and buildings of architectural merit, will provide the visitor to Glasgow with much to see and do. Come and see for yourself – Glasgow's proud boast is indeed that 'Glasgow's Miles Better.' It proves the ideal centre for touring and relaxing, whether this be in city, in the country, or on the coast. The local Strathclyde surburban rail network will enhance any visit to this 'capital' of Strathclyde, providing quick and efficient transport to all lowland areas.

MOTHERWELL–COATBRIDGE–
CUMBERNAULD–LARBERT
by Andrew N. Stephen

Although only having a limited Inter-City service, this section of route provides a useful connection northwards from the main line at Motherwell to the other routes in Central Scotland, particularly for freight traffic.

Upon leaving Motherwell, the line branches away to the right from the main line to Glasgow and immediately passes the traction depot where locomotives for the BSC ore trains to Ravenscraig are maintained. The line leads on over a high bridge to the railway yards at Mossend, where all trains stop for a short time to allow a change of

Scotland's railways are lines for all seasons – a freight train and a local DMU pass each other after heavy snow at Cumbernauld. (*Photo:* William Mcknight)

locomotives, as the overhead wires which have provided electric traction from the South exist for only a few more miles.

The Monklands town of Coatbridge, made prosperous in the eighteenth and nineteenth centuries through coal and the discovery of ironstone, is, after several years in decline, undergoing a remarkable renaissance with the promotion of its industrial heritage. To the north of the town is the container terminal which serves the entire west of Scotland. It is in this area that we traverse part of the route of one of Scotland's oldest railways, the Monklands & Kirkintilloch, which carried the coal to the Forth and Clyde Canal.

Heading now into relatively open country, we can see in the middle distance to the left the carcass of the closed steel rolling mill at Gartcosh. The railway line which passes the works now rejoins us and we share the tracks with the local rail service from Glasgow Queen Street and Springburn to the New Town of Cumbernauld.

Developed from the early 1960s, originally to help solve Glasgow's housing problem, Cumbernauld is now established in its own right and is a flourishing centre for light industry as well as being a pleasant residential and commuter town. Established in 1978 the active Commuter's Association continues to urge the development and improvement of the local DMU train service to and from Glasgow as well as the expansion of all services at Cumbernauld.

Leaving the town through the wooded Vault Glen, it is difficult to imagine that its northern suburbs are high above. After passing through the short Abronhill Tunnel, observe to the left the graceful Castlecary Viaduct carrying the main Glasgow–Edinburgh line which we then pass under to cross into Central Region. Running parallel to the Forth and Clyde Canal and almost exactly along the course of the Roman Antonine Wall, we approach the junction at Greenhill Lower, where the line from Glasgow to Stirling and Perth joins from the right. (For a continuation, see Glasgow–Dundee section, on page 00).

EDINBURGH–STIRLING
By Douglas Smart

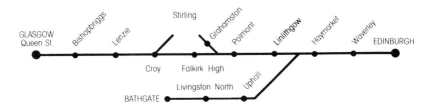

The railway between Edinburgh and Stirling traverses a broad lowland region flanked by the Firth of Forth on the east and by the Campsie Fells on the west. The region bears the scars of not only several centuries of strife with its numerous castles and battlefields, but also several decades of relative industrial decline with its equally numerous derelict mines, foundries, factories, canals, and railways. Both of these aspects of the region's past may be glimpsed from the train.

Rail services between Edinburgh and Stirling operate at half-hourly intervals during the daytime and at hourly intervals in the evening.

Our 36¼-mile journey begins at Edinburgh's vast Waverley Station, which lies in a valley separating the Old and New Towns. The railway runs along the bed of the Nor

Loch, which was drained in the late eighteenth century when the New Town was planned.

A tunnel takes the line under the western extension of the New Town to Haymarket Station, the former terminus of both the Caledonian Railway and the line between Edinburgh and Glasgow. Murryfield international rugby football stadium can be seen on the left about a mile farther on.

At Ratho Junction, immediately after the M8 motorway crosses the line, the Bathgate branch diverges from the left. This line was closed to passenger trains in 1956 but reopened in 1986 – one of the few complete lines to be reopened in Britain in recent years. It was always an important freight line, serving as it did the former British Leyland works at Bathgate, and passenger usage of it has so far been encouraging.

From both the main line and the Bathgate branch can be seen a number of very large red bings (spoil heaps). These are relics of the shale-oil industry, which flourished in West and Mid Lothian from the early nineteenth to the mid twentieth century.

Shortly after passing Ratho Junction, we cross Thomas Telford's thirty-six-arch viaduct over the River Almond. On the right a mile away stands prominently the ruined Niddrie Castle, which is now being restored. Here Mary Queen of Scots spent her first night after escaping from Loch Leven Castle where she was imprisoned.

For the next 14 miles the railway closely follows the Union Canal, which can be seen on the left. Opened in 1822, the Union Canal completed the waterway link between Edinburgh and Glasgow by joining the Forth and Clyde Canal near Falkirk; it was closed to commercial traffic in 1933.

On the approach to Linlithgow a round tower on a hill distinguishes the Binns, a fortified house dating mainly from the seventeenth century (though parts of its are earlier) now owned by the National Trust for Scotland. The Binns is the ancestral home of the Dalyell family, whose most illustrious member was 'General Tam' (1599–1685), a Royalist, who was captured at Worcester, escaped from the Tower of London, reorganised the Tsar's army in Russia, defeated the Covenanters in 1666 at Rullion Green, and in 1681 raised the Scots Greys. The Trust's present tenant is his namesake, the MP for Linlithgow.

Linlithgow is one of David I's royal burghs, with a population of about 5,000. Immediately adjacent to the station stands the thirteenth-century Church of St Michael with its controvesial silver-coloured timber spire erected in 1964 to replace an open stone crown removed in 1821. Behind it lie the ruins of Linlithgow Palace, which was for several centuries a royal residence and the birthplace of Mary Queen of Scots and James V.

The line to Glasgow diverges at Polmont, just under 5 miles from Linlithgow, and keeps to higher ground affording fine views of the Forth Valley and the distant Grampians. It is a superb example of railway-engineering, having been conceived as a fast route from the outset in 1842, and is now the most important route entirely within ScotRail's domain.

Stirling trains take the lower line through Falkirk Grahamston. Descending from the higher ground along an embankment, we cross the line of the Antonine Wall.

Falkirk, a town with about 40,000 inhabitants, gave its name to two battles – in 1298 and 1746. Later its coal-mines and iron-foundries played a significant role in transforming the economy of the Central Lowlands during the Industrial Revolution. In particular, the Carron Iron Works, established in 1760, became famous after 1776 for the manufacture of a new light naval gun known as a 'carronade', which was subsequently used by many navies. Sadly, the firm recently went into liquidation; it began life producing cast-iron stoves and grates and ended it producing bathroom fittings and stainless-steel kitchen sinks.

The newly-modernised Linlithgow station. (*Photo:* British Rail)

Just to the west of Grahamston Station we cross in turn the Forth and Clyde Canal and the site of a Roman fort, and, at Larbert, join the main line from Glasgow to Aberdeen and Inverness.

As our train makes its way across the flat carse of the Forth, the Ochils are prominent on the right. Those seated at the front of a DMU are given an unobscured view directly ahead of Stirling Castle rising conspicuously above the plain.

Stirling with a population of 30,000 is one of Scotland's oldest royal burghs, the title having been conferred on it in 1100. It occupies a commanding position on rising ground above the River Forth – of which it was long the lowest bridging point – and its castle even more so, sited on a 350-foot-high promontory. The castle itself is a remarkably fine example of Renaissance architecture, most of its principal buildings dating from the fifteenth and sixteenth centuries. The Great Hall, which was built for James IV in about 1500, is now being painstakingly restored, having been extensively damaged when the castle was used as a barracks by the Argyll and Sutherland Highlanders. Other places of note in and around Stirling include the Church of the Holy Rude, a fine Gothic building situated at the bottom of Castle Wynd; the Wallace Monument, which contains, among other armorial exhibits, the patriot's two-handed sword; and the Bannockburn Heritage Centre, situated on the supposed site of the battlefield where in 1314 the forces of Robert Bruce routed those of Edward II – the two last-named venues can easily be reached by bus from the station.

Stirling Station is of interest, too, being a Listed building, the front of which bears the crest of the Caledonian Railway Company. Like many other buildings in the town, the station has been carefully restored; and in summer its floral displays delight thousands of visitors. Stirling is also a Motorail terminal.

BATHGATE: A BRANCH OF THE ARTS
by John Yellowlees

The Bathgate branch's claim to fame as the first complete inter-urban rail link reopened to passengers in Britain since the war may not necessarily appeal to the pleasure traveller, but within its 10 miles there is in fact much to see which illustrates the industrial evolution of West Lothian.

Built in 1849, the branch came into existence a decade after the main high-speed Edinburgh–Glasgow line of the North British Railway from which it diverges at Newbridge Junction. Its extension westwards to Airdrie and Glasgow was completed in 1870, and it served the coal and steel industries as well as the important shale-oil industry which had begun with James 'Paraffin' Young opening the world's first oil refinery just south of Bathgate a year before the railway reached the town. It was this industry which would soon leave an indelible mark on the landscape with its mighty red bings or tips. Passenger trains were sparse, the last scheduled service being withdrawn from Bathgate on 7 January 1956.

The decline of the old rail service was matched by the decay of the Scottish shale-oil industry, as competition from imported oil steadily eroded its position. The area's economic salvation was decreed to lie in the wide area round the old village of Livingston becoming Scotland's fourth New Town; while Government intervention persuaded Leyland to site a new truck and tractor plant at Bathgate.

Things do not always work out as planned, however, and while Livingston throve on high technology, the Leyland plant never prospered. By the time its closure was announced in 1984, its rail siding and that to the surviving Balbardie steelworks had been severed so as to improve access for road distributor vehicles to the all-important car railhead. Also lost was the line west to Airdrie, closed to freight and lifted in 1982, while the old Bathgate Upper Station had by then been gutted by an arsonist.

The rest is well known. The change to a more positive railway attitude summarised in the emergence of the title ScotRail just preceded the report of a Government-led working party which recommended the reopening of a rail link to Edinburgh as a speedy and cost-effective means of putting Bathgate on the map for new industry and of attracting the commuters whose presence in other rail-served towns such as Linlithgow had ensured continuing prosperity.

Obstacles of railway accounting were constructively overcome, and such was the enthusiasm generated among the funding partners – the District and Regional Councils, Livingston Development Corporation, and the Scottish Development Agency with European Regional Development fund support – that ScotRail was actually willing to let contracts for station construction even before the respective contributions had been tied up legally.

The hourly service which the Secretary of State for Scotland formally inaugurated on 24 March 1986 normally runs from Platform 15 of Edinburgh Waverley Station and follows the same route as trains to Stirling and Glasgow Queen Street, as far as the old Ratho Station which had closed in 1951, after which the branch veers slightly left alongside a quarry, then straight ahead while the main line swings away to the right. Beneath passes the M8 motorway on which Glasgow-bound drivers can accelerate away from the congestion which surrounds the nearby Newbridge roundabout.

The mastery of the railway pioneers is well demonstrated in the magnificent view which the Bathgate train now affords on Grainger and Miller's superb 1842 Grade A listed Almond Valley Viaduct. On passing several modern industrial premises, the Bathgate line has its own Grade B listed viaduct over the Almond, Birdsmill, after which a much more modern structure takes the line again across the M8.

Within its 75 m.p.h. speed limit, the DMU can sometimes now race cars and coaches (whose limit should be somewhat lower!) on the parallel M8. A third mode of inter-city transport is soon crossed – the Union Canal whose nearby Almond Aqueduct is the third largest in Britain and whose economic destruction at the hands of the railways long preceded official closure in 1959: but whose restoration for enjoyment and leisure purposes are now progressing apace.

To the north, beyond the urban swathe of Broxburn and Uphall in the Vale of Strathbrock, can be seen the long flat bings of the shale-oil industry, which are often reminiscent of the mesas and buttes of America's Wild West; and at this distance one can perhaps appreciate why one of them, the bing now known as 'Niddry Woman', has been hailed as Britain's largest man-made work of art in John Latham's *Art Within Reach*, published by Thames & Hudson. As the train passes on to single track to approach Uphall Station, the bings come close to the line and its motorway neighbour.

'Welcome to Uphall Station', says the ScotRail sign beyond the new car park, for Uphall Station was really a separate community that grew up around the station which, in the days before feeder buses and park and ride, purported to serve the town of that name, over a mile to the north. The station's original name of Houston commemorated the sixteenth-century mansion, now enjoying a splendid reputation as a country hotel, which can be seen down that road.

The train swings away from the M8 to pass warehouses and the modern Cameron iron works which mark the start of Livingston New Town. Modern housing and landscaped open space overlook the train, with a golf-course and the small peak of Dechmont Law to the north, as it passes under several bridges to draw alongside the platform of Livingston North, adjoining the Carmondean shopping centre.

Unlike Uphall, this station is on an entirely new site. The original Livingston Station was about a mile west in what is now the village of Deans, whose residents have to cope with a trek to Livingston North for a train. Perhaps the sculptures of giant feet marking a footpath to the right as the train leaves the station are intended to signify their plight!

An attractive view opens up to the south across shelter belts to the Pentland Hills and another artistically contoured shale bing, the aptly named Five Sisters (see page 00), as the train crosses the Carmondean Burn on track that again doubles so as to give a separate running line for the car trains. On the south side of the line, willow and bog-cotton announce the Tailend Moss, one of the largest surviving areas of lowland bog in the south of Scotland.

A nest of overbridges looms up as the M8 appears from nowhere to get a chance at last to cross the railway. Beyond meadows to the right, houses scale the edge of the upturned wave form that is the Bathgate Hills, while to the left in due course a glimpse can be caught of the old Leyland factory, which awaits reuse, possibly as a shopping and leisure complex. The car terminal then opens out on the left with a golf-course beyond, while to the right the buildings of St Mary's Academy dominate the street scene beyond the infant conifers which now screen the old coal-yard.

When suddenly the train runs within sight of the buffers, there are still one or two surprises to greet the traveller. Conceived as an unstaffed station in contrast to its predecessor, the new Bathgate passenger station has none of its cluttered user-hostile isolation; for the landscaping and continental-inspired red mushroom-like shelters ensure minimal separation from the purpose-built car park and bus turning-circle which are now an integral part of the town centre.

The hostelry facing the new station bears its traditional name of Railway Tavern, as if those who created it knew that this spot was predestined to host a revived railway. Tradition is recalled in the themes which unite a metal screen beyond the passenger track with banners and designs on the railward side of the hoardings in the centre of the car and bus park. The bright green and yellow motifs created on each of these by artists Sam Ainsley and Arthur Watson commemorate the celebratory arches of spruce and flowers erected every June on the houses of children taking part in the annual procession. This recalls the origin of the Stewart dynasty, and has since 1843 marked the benefaction by John Newlands which enabled the establishment of the renowned Bathgate Academy.

For transport conoisseurs as for planners seeking an early revival of the town's economic fortunes, the Bathgatge Railway reopening is in itself something of a work of art. How appropriate, therefore, that the line is worth riding for the sake of those other works of art – the accidentally majestic Victorian shale bings and the specially commissioned features of what is truly a designer terminus.

EDINBURGH–DUNDEE
by Anthony Kay

The railway from Edinburgh to Dundee forms part of Scotland's East Coast Main Line and, therefore, carries fast trains – on the Edinburgh–Aberdeen and London–Aberdeen services – as well as local services. The latter may be subdivided into three groups.

First, an hourly Edinburgh–Dundee service (generally two-hourly on Sundays, with also some two-hourly gaps on weekdays) stopping at Haymarket, Inverkeithing, and all stations from Kirkcaldy to Dundee (though Springfield has only a limited service).

Second, an hourly Edinburgh–Kirkcaldy service, stopping at all stations. This service does not run on Sundays and weekday evenings; at those times Edinburgh–Dundee trains stop at all stations between Inverkeithing and Kirkcaldy.

Third, an hourly Edinburgh–Cowdenbeath service which also stops at stations between Edinburgh and Inverkeithing, but does not run on Sundays. Thus these stations have a half-hourly service on weekdays (hourly in the evenings). On Sundays Dalmeny is served by Edinburgh–Dundee trains.

The frequency of the services south of Kirkcaldy is increased at peak periods, and the major stations are also served by some of the fast trains bound for Aberdeen. The total journey time is about ninety minutes for the 59 miles from Edinburgh to Dundee, and about fifty minutes for the 26-mile Edinburgh–Kirkcaldy service.

The usual arrival and departure platforms at Edinburgh Waverley Station are numbers 17, 18, and 19 for trains going to Dundee, Kirkcaldy, and Aberdeen respectively. All trains stop at Haymarket (Platform 2 northbound, Platform 1 southbound) serving the west end of Edinburgh.

Beyond the Haymarket locomotive sheds there is a junction at which our northbound train parts company with those travelling west towards Glasgow and Stirling. The international rugby football ground at Murryfield is passed on the right, with the wooded Corstorphine Hill behind it, while a wider panorama of the Pentland Hills opens up on the left. The next station is South Gyle, an unmanned halt opened in 1985 to serve an area of new housing on the western edge of Edinburgh. Beyond this, we pass Edinburgh's Turnhouse Airport before arriving at Dalmeny Station, which also serves South Queensferry. There are many pleasant rambles possible in Dalmeny Park to the east and Hopetoun Park to the west; these parks are the grounds of stately homes – Dalmeny House and Hopetoun House – which are open to the public during the tourist season.

Beyond Dalmeny, the train crosses what is probably the most famous and distinctive railway structure in Britain: the Forth Bridge. Built for strength rather than beauty, construction commenced in 1882 just three years after the Tay Bridge Disaster. The bridge contains 54,000 tons of steel, 21,000 tons of cement, and 140,000 cubic yards of masonry. It cost £3,250,000 (and the lives of fifty-seven workmen) and was opened by HRH The Prince of Wales on 4 March 1890. The track is 158 feet above the high-water mark, and on a clear day there are excellent views over the countryside of Fife to the north and West Lothian and the Forth Road Bridge to the west. This suspension bridge replaced the last ferry across the Forth at Queensferry when it opened in 1964; the first ferry had been instituted by Queen Margaret in the eleventh century, to carry pilgrims to Dunfermline.

At the north end of the Forth Bridge is North Queensferry Station, beyond which further feats of engineering were required to take the railway the next 2 miles inland: there is a tunnel and a deep cutting through the hard volcanic rock of the Ferry Hills, followed by the Jamestown Viaduct and another tunnel, before the line emerges at Inverkeithing Station. The branch coming in from the right just before the station is from Rosyth Naval Dockyard.

Inverkeithing is a particularly busy station, since many Abderdeen-bound fast trains stop here as well as the local services. On Sundays it also acts as the railhead for Dunfermline. The main station building on the northbound side was completely rebuilt in 1985–86, and is, therefore, one of the most modern in Scotland.

Trains bound for Cowdenbeath or Cardenden turn left at the junction to the north of Inverkeithing, while we bear right to travel parallel to the coast. The railway passes an industrial estate at Dalgety Day, a small New Town for which it is hoped a station may be opened in the near future. The next existing station is at Aberdour, an attractive seaside town which from April to September is also the departure point for the ferry to Inchcolm Island, on which are situated the twelfth-century St Colm's Abbey and some old fortifications. Aberdour Station is notable for its floral display, and the remains of Aberdour Castle may be seen just beyond on the right.

About ½ mile beyond Aberdour, the railway meets the shore of the Firth of Forth at Silversands Bay. Between here and Kirkcaldy, there are good views over the Forth, the main landmarks being Arthur's Seat and the Pentland Hills behind Edinburgh, Inchkeith Island and, farther east, North Berwick Law and the Bass Rock. The more immediate scenery is also quite dramatic between Aberdour and Burntisland, as the railway cuts across a steep wooded slope above the shoreline.

Entering Burntisland from the west, we see its less attractive side: a chemical factory on the left, and then the docks on the right. These docks are now much less busy than in the late nineteenth century, when Burntisland was the major port for the shipment of Fife's coal. The harbour had also been the terminal for the railway from 1847 until the Forth Bridge was opened: passengers from Edinburgh to Fife and beyond had taken a ferry from Granton to Burntisland before continuing northwards by train. A plaque on the northbound platform commemorates Burntisland's important place in railway history.

A better view of the town of Burntisland is seen beyond the station, as the railway skirts a park; the very steep hill behind the town is The Binn (636 feet). The railway continues to hug the rocky coastline as far as Pettycur Harbour, before entering Kinghorn Tunnel, notable for the kink near its western end. Kinghorn Station is reached soon after leaving the tunnel.

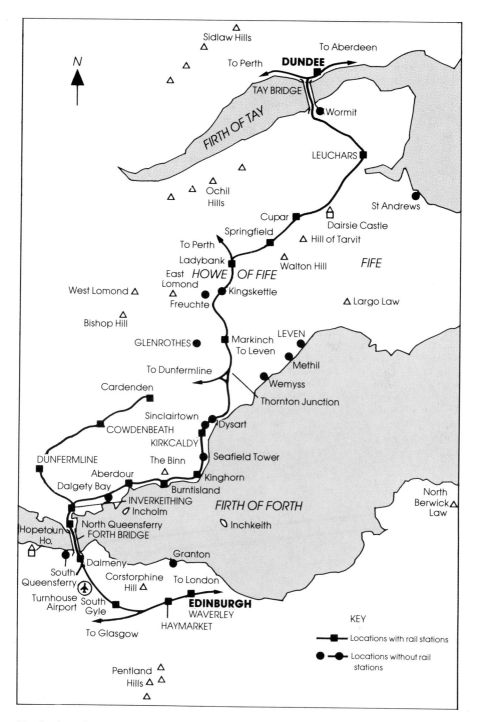

Map showing rail network between Edinburgh and Dundee

Continuing along the coast, we pass the ruined Seafield Tower, before Seafield Colliery reminds us that coal-mining has traditionally been the major industry in this part of Fife. The railway gradually climbs and moves inland as it enters Kirkcaldy, the largest town in Fife with a population of 50,000, passing Raith Rovers football ground on the right and Beveridge Park on the left. The station is situated close to the town centre, and is particularly convenient for the Adam Smith Centre, a venue for a wide variety of entertainments and meetings. Most of the fast trains from London or Edinburgh to Aberdeen stop at Kirkcaldy. Beyond the station the railway passes various factories (Kirkcaldy is noted for the manufacture of linoleum) and the sites of former stations at Sinclairtown and Dysart, before turning northwards and inland.

At Thornton Junction, nothing now remains of what was once one of the busiest stations in Scotland, and nature is reclaiming the derelict land. The line going eastwards to Wemyss has been dismantled, but those going west towards Dunfermline and north-east to Levenmouth serving Methil Docks and Levenmouth power-station are still open to goods traffic. There is also one early-morning passenger train from Markinch to Edinburgh via Dunfermline. The last passenger trains to Leven were in 1969; however, this line served a sizeable population and deserves to be reopened to passenger traffic, while the line westwards from Thornton Junction could be used to provide better connections between Kirkcaldy and north-east Fife to stations between Dunfermline and Cardenden.

Continuing northwards, we can see the Lomond Hills and Bishop Hill on the left, and the conspicuous double summit of Largo Law on the right. The next station is Markinch, which also serves the new town of Glenrothes, 2 miles to the west. Since 1974 Glenrothes, with a population of some 30,000, has been the administrative headquarters of Fife Region; it is connected to Markinch Station by a frequent bus service.

North of Markinch, we pass through the gap between the Lomond Hills and the East Fife plateau to enter the Howe of Fife. This is a roughly triangular area of flat land dominated by the north-facing escarpment of the Lomond Hills; before the eighteenth century it consisted mainly of wild heathland and bogs, but since being drained it has been given over to agriculture and forestry, mainly pine. Thus, while there are several old settlements round the edge of the Howe, those in its interior are more recent.

One such settlement is Ladybank, the next stop on the line; though we pass within ½ mile of Freuchie, and go through Kingskettle, on the way. The town of Ladybank grew up round the railway junction in the nineteenth century. The line westwards to Kinross no longer exists, but the branch that continues northwards to Perth still carries some passenger traffic. However, our journey takes us eastwards through pine woods to Springfield and Cupar.

Springfield is an unmanned halt with a less-frequent service than the other stations on this line – only five trains in each direction stop here each weekday mostly during peak commuting periods, and the station is closed on Sundays. Beyond Springfield the sixteenth-century Scotstarvit Tower is visible on the skyline to the right, in the dip between Walton Hill and the Hill of Tarvit. Near by, but not visible from the railway, is the National Trust for Scotland's Hill of Tarvit Mansion, open to the public.

The next station is at Cupar, formerly the county town of Fife with a population of 7,000. This pleasant town, with its market cross of 1683, would make a good base for exploring the north-east Fife countryside by bicycle; there is a good network of quiet lanes, and plenty of variety in the scenery. The railway leaves Cupar down the Eden Valley, passing the remains of Dairsie Castle – partly concealed among the trees – on the right after three miles. Dairsie Church is close by, but the village is nearly a mile away on the hillside to the left. As we approach Leuchars, a prominent landmark on the left is a large quarry of pink stone on the side of Lucklaw Hill.

On arrival at Leuchars, one may be forgiven for wondering why a station serving a small village should have so many fast trains stopping, as well as all local services. The answer may be deduced from the signs announcing 'Alight here for St Andrews'. Scotland's oldest university town, famed also as the home of golf, is 5 miles away, and Leuchars has been its railhead since 1969 when the line to St Andrews was closed. There are now frequent buses (every half hour on weekdays, hourly on Sundays), and there are usually taxis waiting outside Leuchars Station when trains arrive.

As well as its golf-courses, St Andrews has many other tourist attractions: these include the ruins of its cathedral and castle, many other notable buildings, and the 2-mile length of the West Sands, one of the finest beaches on the east coast of Scotland.

Leuchars itself is best known for its Romanesque church and for its RAF base, which plays a significant role in Britain's defences. Quite near the village is Earlshall Castle, recently opened to the public and noted for its topiary gardens.

Beyond Leuchars, the railway passes several sand and gravel quarries on its way to Wormit at the southern end of the Tay Bridge. Wormit lost its station when the branch line to Newport closed in 1969, but a local action group has been pressing for a new station which it is hoped will be built on the main line. The present Tay Bridge, with eighty-five spans covering a total length of 2 miles and 364 yards, was opened in 1887, replacing Thomas Bouch's bridge which collapsed disastrously in the storm of 28 December 1879 with great loss of life. The old bridge had only lasted two years, and the stumps of its piers still remain, close to the piers of the present bridge.

The views from the Tay Bridge are on the south of the river Ochil and on the north the Sidlaw Hills with the Tay Road Bridge, opened in 1966, to the right. Before reaching the northern shore, the rail bridge curves to the right, so that the railway is aligned parallel to the river bank when it descends to join the line from Perth for the final ½ mile into Dundee Station. This station has bar and buffet facilities, and is only a few minutes' walk from the city centre.

The prosperity of Dundee – Scotland's fourth largest city with a population of about 200,000 – was largely founded on the jute industry. Although it has suffered as a result of the decline of its traditional industry, it remains a lively city, with good shopping facilities, a university and a college of technology, two very successful football teams and a busy port. Captain Scott's ship, HMS Discovery, now has a permanent home in Dundee's harbour, and can be visited by the public. The hinterland of Angus and East Perthshire is accessible by bus (the bus station is on the east side of the town centre), and there are rail connections up the coast towards Aberdeen.

LADYBANK–PERTH
by Anthony Kay

The single-track railway on the Edinburgh–Dundee line from Ladybank to Perth was reopened to passenger traffic in 1975, after a period of twenty years as a freight-only line. There are presently two trains a day in each direction with only one train on Sundays; at Perth they connect with trains on the Highland line to Inverness, while at the other end of the line the journeys start and finish beyond Ladybank, at Edinburgh or Kirkcaldy. Connections to and from Cupar and Leuchars may be made at Ladybank.

This line is one of the most under-used passenger railways in Scotland, not merely because it carries infrequent trains, but because it passes through three substantial settlements which at present have no station. If the stations at Newburgh, Abernethy,

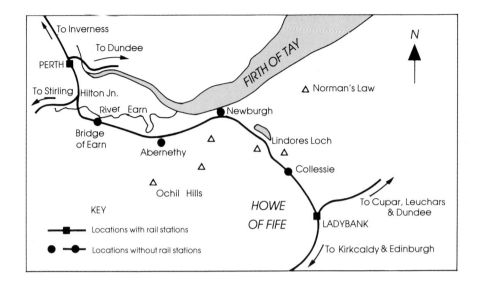

and Bridge of Earn were reopened, they would probably generate sufficient traffic to justify a more frequent service. Nevertheless, the line does provide a useful connection from Fife to Perth and the Highlands, and is itself of considerable scenic interest.

The first 3 miles from Ladybank to Collessie are across the flat Howe of Fife, but the line then enters the Ochil Hills by way of Collessie Den, a narrow and steep-sided valley. The views are of grassy or bracken-covered and occasionally wooded hillsides rising steeply on both sides until we emerge on the shore of Londores Loch. Beyond the loch can be seen Norman's Law, at 935 feet the highest hill in North Fife, which is crowned by the remains of an Iron Age hill-fort.

Continuing above the Den of Lindores and past Clatchard Craig Quarry, a panorama of the Firth of Tay and the Sidlaw Hills opens out on our right; immediately below us now is the town of Newburgh, stretched out along its main street. The former station is towards the west end of the town, and some of the station buildings survive, though in a derelict state.

The railway continues along the base of the Ochils' northern escarpment to Abernethy, famous for its 74-foot-high Pictish round tower. Abernethy was an ecclesiastical centre of national importance a thousand years ago, but it is now a small and quiet town. The platforms of the old station are still in place, but none of the station buildings remain.

From here, the railway strikes out across a broad plain between the River Earn and the Ochils, to pass under the M90 motorway and through Bridge of Earn. This village has expanded considerably in recent years and now has a population of about 2,000. After crossing the River Earn a mile north-west of the village, we join the main line from Stirling at Hilton Junction and then enter Moncrieffe Tunnel (1,180 yards long). From the northern end of this tunnel, it is little more than a mile to Perth Station, situated adjacent to the town's bus station and a few minutes' walk from the town centre. The 18-mile journey from Ladybank takes about twenty-five minutes, slow enough to enable us to enjoy the varied scenery *en route*.

EDINBURGH–GLASGOW CENTRAL
by Bill Russell

While most passengers travel from Scotland's capital to its largest city by fast ScotRail express (leaving Edinburgh on the hour and on the half-hour) which reaches Glasgow in forty-eight minuts, few choose the more leisurely, though no less interesting, journey via West Calder and Shotts. Instead of the air-conditioned comfort of the push-pull service on the original North British Railway route through Falkirk, our stopping DMU will take us over the more hilly former Caledonian (or Caley) route taking one and a half hours to cover the 46¼ miles. While the trains may not be the most modern, the line enjoys for the most part an hourly service, coinciding with the opening of Livingston South Station, the first to serve the expanding New Town; and some of the stations are starting-points for exploration by bicycle or by bus. In terms of speed and comfort the Caley route to Glasgow Central takes second place to the 100 m.p.h. route to Glasgow Queen Street. But this was not always so: there was great rivalry between the two companies last century and also between them and the canals.

The Edinburgh & Glasgow Railway (E & G) through Falkirk opened in 1842 with its terminus at Haymarket. In 1846, the extension to the North British Station (now Waverley) was completed.

In 1848, the Caledonian Railway from Carlisle reached Carstairs where it branched to Glasgow and to Edinburgh. The next year the Caley started to compete with the E & G by running trains to Glasgow via Carstairs, Motherwell, Coatbridge, and by the Garnkirk & Glasgow Railway metals to Buchanan Street, a distance of 58¾ miles – 11 miles longer than the E & G route. When the Caley ran four non-stop tains in two hours, the Edinburgh & Glasgow Railways countered with four trains, each taking one and a half hours.

To win passengers, a fare-cutting war broke out and it cost only sixpence (2½p) to travel between the two cities for through passengers only – it cost up to one third more if you joined the trains at intermediate stations.

By 1870 there were fifty-four trains travelling mostly empty each way between the two cities operated by the Caley and the North British Railway companies, the latter having taken over the E & G. By 1886 the 9 a.m. to Glasgow Central took sixty-five minutes while today it takes thirty minutes longer as there are no express trains on the route, a far cry from the early twentieth century when Pullman cars were often attached to the trains.

In the modernised travel centre at Edinburgh Waverley, notice the magnificent ceiling of the original building before proceeding to Platform 13 for our three-coach DMU. British Rail wanted to drop the name 'Waverley' – taken from Sir Walter Scott's novels – to fit in with national policy of using only the town name where only one station existed; but the capital's citizens objected and Scotland's busiest station remains 'Waverley'.

On leaving Waverley, on our right we pass the 61 metre high monument to Sir Walter Scott before entering the tunnel beneath two art galleries, built in the Classical style – the Royal Scottish Academy and the National Gallery. On our left the Castle, guarding the top of the Royal Mile, stands on the site of a Pictish settlement later to be occupied by King Edwin of Northumbria, perhaps the reason for the name Edinburgh (Edwin's burgh). Many historical acts have taken place within the Castle walls, which house the Honours of Scotland – the Crown, the Sceptre, and the Sword of State. The rock itself is an extinct volcanic plug with the Royal Mile utilising what geographers call the crag-and-tail formation. The annual Military Tattoo is held on the Castle Esplanade, about the same time (August–September) as the Edinburgh International Festival of Music and Drama which started in 1947. It is from the battlements that the 'one-o'clock gun' is fired daily.

The road called 'The Mound' under which we have passed was built on rubble left when the Georgian New Town of Edinburgh, north of Princes Street was constructed.

In Princes Street Gardens on the right there is a world-famous floral clock. At the top of The Mound is the Assembly Hall in which is held the Annual General Assembly of the Church of Scotland. Originally the line through the gardens was double track, but this caused severe congestion (expresses from the north could take up to two hours to complete the last few miles), and so in 1901 an expanded station at Waverley was built, the track was quadrupled, and extra tunnels built at The Mound and at Haymarket.

Before entering Haymarket Tunnel under Lothian Road, there are two buildings of note, one small and one large. On the right in the graveyard of St Cuthbert's Church is a small tower used by relatives of the departed to keep a watch for 'Resurrectionists', a body of men who exhumed corpses and sold them for medical research. The majestic building on Lothian Road would have been our departure station until September 1965 as it was the Caledonian's terminus called 'Princes Street Station'. As long ago as 1845 a grand terminal building was promised but the original station remained and was little more than a wooden shanty on Lothian Road. A fire in 1890 in the expanded, but still temporary, buildings hastened the erection of the stone edifice which later incorporated the Caledonian Hotel. The station had seven platforms at street-level and was opened in 1893. Although only a small crowd gathered to await the arrival of the last train from Glasgow just after midnight on Sunday, 5 September 1965, many travellers missed the friendliness of the staff of the Caley. In latter years the 2245 Saturdays-only departure for Glasgow contained a large proportion of inebriated passengers and the staff would sometimes advise people to return by the 2154 service if they thought the passengers were abstainers. One porter stated to a lady, 'Madam, the 2154 is the sociable train; the 2245 is the joyful.' The route of the Western Approach Road follows the trackbed of the former Caley Railway.

Just under four minutes from leaving Waverley we emerge at the modernised Haymarket Station. The street-level buildings were to be replaced by a multi-storey office block, but after a balloon was flown to the height of the proposed building, residents and councillors decided that the skyline would be spoiled and, instead, the original building has been cleaned and refurbished.

We leave the main E & G line noting on the right the turrets of Donaldson's School for the Deaf and then the Haymarket motive power depot. It was this Duff Street connection which allowed Princes Street and Merchiston stations to close and our train to be routed from Waverley. We pass under a branch of the Western Approach

Opposite: A 100 mph ScotRail express on the main Edinburgh to Glasgow line. (*Photo:* British Rail)

Road, a former railway line, and we can see the floodlights of Heart of Midlothian's football ground on the right at Tynecastle, and Gorgie Children's Farm to our left. As we cross the suburban Circle railway, the subject of a reopening proposal and the scene in December of popular Santa specials, we join the original route from Princes Street Station on our left at Slateford Junction, where the redundant signal-box has been converted into a functional part of the Signal and Telecommunications Training School.

The eight-arched aqueduct on our left takes the Union Canal from its terminus at Fountainbridge on its way to Falkirk where it links up with the Forth and Clyde Canal. The branch line to Balerno built to serve the mills on the Water of Leith and provide a passenger service from Currie and Juniper Green also is just discernible. Passengers travelled in shorter coaches necessitated by the twisty nature of the track which follows the Water of Leith – now the route is a popular walkway and nature trail.

Kingsknowe was reopened in 1971, having been closed in 1964.

Due south are the Pentland Hills on which there is an artificial ski slope at Hillend. The large housing area of Wester Hailes has its own station opened in May 1987. After which we cross part of the city bypass, now in its final stages of completion. From the

One of Scotland's new stations – Livingston South, with passengers about to board a train for Edinburgh. (*Photo:* Bill Russell)

The Glasgow–Edinburgh train in West Calder's neat station. (*Photo:* Bill Russell)

back of the train can be seen the Edinburgh skyline of the Castle Rock and Arthur's Seat with its 'sleeping lion' outline, both of which are the remains of extinct volcanoes.

We emerge from a cutting at Curriehill Station reopened in September 1987. The Heriot-Watt University campus is out of sight to our right, so were the houses of Currie when Curriehall Station was originally in use but since then houses and schools have appeared over the horizon and the trains stop here once more.

After a straight stretch, the line formation of the Balerno loop can be seen on the left joining us at Ravelrig Junction. Latterly the sidings here were used for stabling the Royal Train overnight. The hard rock of Dalmahoy and Kaimes Hills are of similar origin to the Castle Rock. Remains of an Iron Age fort have been found here.

As the train emerges from a cutting, a panorama of the eastern part of the central belt comes into view: on a clear day you can see the Firth of Forth and the Fife Hills, the Forth Road and Rail bridges and the bings of West Lothian.

Closer to the railway on the right are the cream-coloured, brown-roofed houses of the war-blinded ex-servicemen at Linburn. Near Kirknewton Station, the houses which overlook the railway were built for the American Air Force personnel who worked at the base near here – the higher the rank, the higher up the hill stood the house. Later the Black Watch at Ritchie Camp occupied the houses but this is now

27

closed. The station changed its name from Midcalder (the village is 3 miles away) to Kirknewton in 1982. The train climbs to Midcalder Junction where we leave the Carstairs route, for the 'short cut' to Glasgow, opened in 1869, which allowed the Caledonian to compete with the North British on more favourable terms for the Edinburgh – Glasgow traffic. Livingston New Town has expanded over the years but had its first taste of rail travel in October 1984 when the new station of Livingston South was opened with its bus connection to the town centre. The hourly train service is the best this section of the line has ever had. The inclusion of 'South' in the station name suggested that a second station would serve the town and in 1986 the railway to Bathgate reopened with the station Livingston North.

Two miles farther on, beside the houses on the right is the site of Limefield Junction from which mineral lines to serve the shale-mines left the main line. There are only four sites near railway property in Scotland where there are Tree Preservation orders – this is one of them.

West Calder Station is arguably the best-kept station on the line, winning first-class prizes for its station gardens. But West Calder has other claims to fame. It has the credit (pardon the pun) of having the first savings bank in Scotland: it was founded by the local Minister, the Reverened John Muckersy in 1807 called the West Calder Friendly Bank. In 1893 West Calder was the first village in Scotland to have street lighting, supplied by the Co-op. The rate-payers did not even have to pay for lampposts as the lights were attached to buildings in the Main Street.

James Young discovered that the shale deposits in the area were ideal for the extraction of crude oil and Young's Paraffin Light and Mineral Oil Company started its Addiewell oil works in 1864. A local historian writes, 'There is no doubt that the rush to erect oil works from 1865 to 1868 led to the Caledonian Railway Company making their Cleland and Mid Calder Branch Line which passes through the parish and has greatly added to its prosperity.' Scottish Oils took over the mines and oil works until, in 1962, the industry closed due to Government withdrawal of the preference tax on crude oil.

As the train climbs slowly from West Calder, the Bathgate Hills lie 5 miles to the north. Much closer are the 'Five Sisters', bings of shale deposited after the crude oil has been extracted: it is proposed to leave these standing as a memorial to 'Paraffin' Young's shale-oil industry. Often the red shale proved useful for road foundations and Addiewell Bing, formerly a 'Table Mountain' of shale, is gradually being removed. Here was the site of Young's Addiewell oil works, the foundation-stone of which was laid by his lifelong friend, the missionary and explorer, David Livingstone. Between West Calder and Shotts, mineral branches left the Caley line for coal, shale, and sand, while the North British pushed railways into this area from the Bathgate – Airdrie line.

Now little more than a platform with a bus shelter, there used to be a waiting-room on the Glasgow side of Addiewell Station heated from the station buildings on the Edinburgh platform by means of a pipe passing under the railway.

The station is isolated now, as the main housing scheme is at Loganlea. A few miles on, the village of Woodmuir is now known by its station name Breich. The observant traveller will notice – or not notice, to his or her cost – the low platforms. When the station was staffed, the railman placed a box near the carriage door to assist the passengers. Despite its rural and rather bleak setting, traffic lights were installed at the crossroads, the scene of many a serious accident. The inhabitants have always wanted the station nearer the village, perhaps more so now as the bus service is very infrequent.

As the railway curves round to Fauldhouse we leave the A71 Edinburgh – Kilmarnock road and on our left glimpse Levenseat sand quarry.

The 'Five Sisters' – shale bings near West Calder. (*Photo:* Bill Russell)

Fauldhouse once boasted two stations as the North British tracks crossed under our route on their way from Bathgate to Morningside: the keen observer can just discern the remains, they lie mainly on the right-hand side of the track.

We leave the last station in Lothian Region on our way to Shotts, in Strathclyde, by way of Benhar Junction, the highest point on the line where the branch to Polkemmet Colliery joins our line. The TV masts at Kirk o' Shotts and Blackhill are a few miles away, beside the M8 motorway.

Shotts was a busy mining town with its ironworks and the evidence of this is still apparent. In severe winters the inhabitants had been grateful for the trains when all the roads had been blocked – one of the reasons for the line's reprieve in the Beeching era. As well as traffic to Edinburgh and Glasgow, there is local traffic between intermediate stations, including the next station Hartwood, serving a tiny village. But the large hospital nearby generates revenue especially on Saturdays.

Between Hartwood and Cleland we can see villages which grew up near the mines and on a clear day, the 707 metre-high Tinto Hill dominates the skyline. On leaving Cleland, the train plunges into a deep cuting, emerging to a view of the BSC works at Ravenscraig.

Carfin was one of the last stations in Scotland to have the title 'Halt' dropped from

29

its name. A few yards from the station on the left is the Grotto, the scene of pilgrimages and processions organised by the Roman Catholic Church. A replica of the Lourdes Shrine, it was built with the help of out-of-work miners in the 1920s.

We are soon under the electric wires, as the loop through Wishaw, a useful diversion from the main line, joins us.

Holytown Station to the casual traveller looks as though it has been abandoned. Vandalism has ruled the day in what was once a busy station with its connecting service to Motherwell and Hamilton. The sharp curve on the left is used by one passenger train each way daily. We cross the main line to the north before the busy Hamilton Circle Railway trails in as we approach Bellshill Station. Trains leave for Motherwell, Hamilton, and Blantyre from here but British Rail do not advertise connections to the Hamilton Circle line.

Leaving Bellshill, we can see Hamilton with the modern Regional Offices, and then on our left the Cathkin Braes. No sooner have we passed under the M74 to Carlisle than we join the main line to Motherwell and the South. Uddingston is a pleasant village on the banks of the Clyde. Most Scots have heard of Tunnock's Caramel Wafer Biscuits which are made here.

The tall lights of Scotland's own – and smaller – 'Spaghetti Junction' at Baillieston

Glasgow Central station after a £3.2 million modernisation programme. (*Photo:* British Rail)

can be seen on the right. The small village of Newton is served by electric trains, but not by ours, as the station is on the line from Blantyre and the line to Glasgow via Kirkhill.

Cambuslang Station is situated in a cutting and is the last station before Glasgow Central. Next to the Rutherglen Station is the ScotRail training school. After Polmadie sheds the railway curves through 90 degrees for its approach to Glasgow's finest railway terminal.

But it was not always such an impressive terminus. Services from Lanarkshire into Glasgow terminated south of the River Clyde until in 1873 an Act gave the go-ahead for the construction of a station on the north bank, the railway approaches being above a widened road bridge at the Broomielaw. By the 1876 Act, it was decided instead to build a new bridge 60 yards downstream and it was completed in 1878, opening the following year along with the new Central Station. The contractor, William Arrol, later built the Tay Bridge, Tower Bridge, and the Forth Bridge. Traffic increased, and by 1901, reconstruction work had begun to enlarge the station. This was completed in 1905, with the internal space and approaches doubled in size. Of the thirteen platforms, Platform 3 was for the Edinburgh trains. The train indicator consisted of boards with the station names served by each train, placed in each of the thirteen windows (above the present booking-office) and was 'of such generous proportions that he who runs (to catch his train) may read without diminishing aught of his haste'. But, sadly, with the 'Electronic Age', it succumbed to the huge electronic departure board.

Resignalling work in 1956 allowed the four tracks on the eastern bridge to be taken out of use leaving six tracks to cater for all the traffic in and out of the high-level station.

So, one and a half hours after leaving Edinburgh, we pull slowly into Glasgow Central, a fitting terminus for Scotland's railway capital.

EXCURSIONS FROM STATIONS ON THE EDINBURGH–GLASGOW RAILWAY

Slateford/Kingsknowe
Water of Leith Walkway – a forty minute walk along part of the old railway route to Balerno.

Kirknewton
Pentland Hills – for the keen hiker.

Almondell and Calderwood Country Park – pleasant country walks through natural woods and areas of daffodils and rhododendrons, rivers spanned by bridges of historical note; visitor centre with aquarium and evolution display. (Telephone Midcalder 882254.)

Livingston South
Bus connection by Eastern Scottish to Livingston town centre.

Almondvale Park – leisure activities, including a trim course, skate-park, and BMX track.

Livingston Mill Farm – restored eighteenth-century farm showing farming of 200 years ago; children welcome to touch the livestock; working seventeenth-century water-mill. Monday–Friday by appointment; Saturday–Sunday 10 a.m. – 5 p.m. (Telephone Livingston 414957.)

West Calder
Access to the Paraffin Young Heritage Trail (by cycle).

Breich
Polkemmet Country Park (by cycle – turn right over railway bridge and follow A706 to Whitburn then 4 miles and a steep hill to Longridge with a panoramic view.) The park is an area of natural beauty with golf-course and a driving practice range. (Telephone Whitburn 43905.)

Shotts
Bus service to Airdrie.

Carfin
Religious grotto, a few yards from the station.

Trains to Motherwell
    Hamilton – most interesting burgh; museum Strathclyde Park; Mausoleum to the Dukes of Hamilton with a fantastic echo.
    Blantyre – birthplace of David Livingstone, the missionary and explorer. His house in Shuttle Row is preserved as a national monument with picnic areas – close to the station.

Bellshill
Bus service to Coatbridge – turn right at station exit and go straight through the cross to the bus shelter on North Road. A Heritage Park is being developed in Coatbridge illustrating the industrial past of the Monklands area.

Uddingston
Bothwell Castle lying 1½ miles from the station is a large building with a cylindrical donjon is in a beautiful setting by the River Clyde. Two miles away is the attractive village of Bothwell with its fifteenth-century church. Another mile brings you to the site of the Battle of Bothwell Bridge where the covenanters were defeated by Monmouth in 1679.

Cambuslang
Trains to Central Low Level via Rutherglen, Bridgeton, Argyle Street, and North Bank suburban stations.

Glasgow Central
Trains to the south, Ayrshire Coast (Stranraer, Ayr, Largs), Wemyss Bay, Gourock (for Clyde steamers); Central Low Level trains on the Argyle line; East Kilbride and the Cathcart Circle.

GLASGOW–DUNDEE
by Douglas Smart

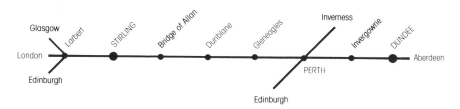

This cross-country route takes us from Scotland's commercial capital to the east coast. Although it is not endowed with the scenic grandeur of the various Highland routes described elsewhere in this book, it does pass through much attractive landscape and gives the traveller an agreeable foretaste of the more dramatic scenery farther north. Trains run between Glasgow and Dundee every two hours, completing the 83¼-mile journey in just under ninety minutes; from Dundee they continue northwards along the Scottish East Coast Main Line to Aberdeen.

Our journey begins at Glasgow's recently modernised Queen Street Station, an edifice distinguished by a fine curved roof. Immediately after departing we enter Cowlairs Tunnel with its steep 1:42 gradient. When the railway first opened in 1842 trains had to be pulled up this incline by a cable attached to a stationary engine because the locomotives of the day were not powerful enough to do so alone.

At Springburn Junction the West Highland line diverges to the left. Springburn was once famous for its locomotive works, which are now but a memory.

After Bishopriggs our route runs along the Kelvin Valley. Running on courses parallel with it about a mile away are the Forth and Clyde Canal and the Antonine Wall. The former, linking Bowling, on the Clyde, with Grangemouth, a distance of 38 miles, was opened in 1790 and, though closed to commercial traffic in 1963, still fulfils a useful role as a recreational waterway. From the train it is best seen just west of Dullator, near the summit of the line.

Nothing of the remains of the Antonine Wall, however, can be seen from the train. This 40 mile-long Roman rampart was erected about AD 142 to restrict the raids of the Northern tribes. Anyone wishing to inspect its remains should alight at Croy and walk north-westwards to Barr Hill and north-eastwards to Croy Hill.

Lenzie, the second station on our route, was developed as a commuter village by the railway company in order to generate more revenue at their new station. Less than a mile to the east of Lenzie we cross the course of one of Scotland's earliest railways, the Monkland & Kirkintilloch Railway, which opened in 1826.

Across the Kelvin Valley there are fine views of the Campsie Fells, the highest point of which is Earl's Seat at 1,896 feet. At Castlecary a viaduct carries the line across the A80 trunk road between Glasgow and Stirling. Immediately east of the viaduct we pass the site of a Roman fort.

At Greenhill the main line from Carstairs and Motherwell comes in from the left and the main line to Edinburgh diverges from the right.

Stirling is our next stop – for a description of the town page 00.

Shortly after leaving Stirling Station we cross the River Forth. On the left beyond the present road bridge is the fifteenth-century Auld Brig. And on the right is the Wallace Monument standing 220 feet high above Abbey Craig rock, itself 362 feet high; the view from the top on a clear day extends as far as Edinburgh and the Forth bridges in the east and Ben Lomond and other mountains in the west.

The new station at Bridge of Allan serves this former spa town, just to the south of which lies the modern campus of the University of Stirling. Our train then ascends a steep gradient through the wooded gorge of Allan Water, whose cataracts can be seen on the right.

On leaving Dunblane Station travellers should not miss the splendid view on the right of Dunblane Cathedral. The lower part of the tower dates from about 1150, and the rest of the building from the thirteenth and fifteenth centuries. Three slabs in the centre of the choir commemorate Margaret Drummond, the secret wife of James IV, who was poisoned by certain noblemen to enable the King to marry Princess Margaret of England.

From Dunblane to Perth – a distance of some 28 miles – there are good views of the Ochils on the right and the foothills of the Grampians on the left. At Gleneagles we can see the V-shaped Glen Eagles, a scenic wooded and moorland glen situated on the edge of the Muir of Ochil. The name has nothing to do with eagles: it derives from the Gaelic word *eaglais* meaning 'church'. Gleneagles itself is renowned for its golf-courses and for its hotel which was until recently railway-owned. Gleneagles Station in fact serves the town of Auchterarder, which was burned down in 1715 on the orders of the Earl of Mar after the Battle of Sheriffmuir in order to deny shelter to the army of the Duke of Argyll. Auchterarder also figures prominently in the history of Protestantism in Scotland.

Situated on a slope on the north side of the valley near the point where the railway joins the River Earn is the House of Gask, the home of Lady Nairne (1766–1845) who wrote many famous Scots songs, including 'The Laird o' Cockpen', 'Will Ye No' Come Back Again', and 'Auld Hoose'.

Perth, our next stop, is an ancient royal burgh with a population of 42,000. But despite its considerable antiquity, few historic buildings survive today. The oldest building in the town is St John's Church, dating from the fifteenth century. Nevertheless, Perth enjoys an attractive setting on the banks of the River Tay between two areas of parkland known as North and South Inch. Indeed, tradition has it that when Agricola's soldiers first set eyes upon the Tay and the South Inch they shouted 'Ecce Tiberis', a comparison to which Sir Walter Scott in 1828 in *The Fair Maid of Perth* scathingly rejoined:

'Behold the Tiber,' the vain Roman cried,
Viewing the ample Tay from Beglie's side;
But where's the Scot what would the vaunt repay,
And hail the puny Tiber for the Tay!

The Fair Maid's house can still be seen today behind Charlotte Street and is open to visitors.

Leaving Perth, which is an important railway junction, our route runs through the carse of Gowrie, a fertile tract of land between the Sidlaw Hills and the Tay noted for its soft fruit. As our train passes close to the edge of Invergowrie Bay (now used as a rubbish dump) there are views Dundee's road and rail bridges.

CITY OF DUNDEE
by Hugh Neville

Coming up from the station platform which lies lower than high water in the nearby Tay Estuary, you cannot help seeing – it is so tall – Tayside Region's headquarters, controlling railway stations as far distant as Gleneagles, Montrose, Blair Atholl, and Rannoch – the last-named being 170 rail miles and over four hours' rail travelling time away, via Glasgow.

To your right, across a busy road – take care – is the start of a riverside promenade going westward to beyond the world's longest – we think – railway bridge over running water. On the other side of the water is Fife. In the reverse direction, towards the sea, is a road bridge which must also be among the world's longest.

But turn round now and push landwards past the station (there are various footbridges, passages, and streets) as far as Nethergate. There you cannot help seeing – it is so tall – the Old Steeple which is in fact of rectangular form (not all words have exactly the same meaning in Scotland as they do in England). When built this lay outside the town, the historic centre now being to your right.

Go that way to City Square with, on two sides of it, the City Chambers housing the City of Dundee District Council and the huge Caird Hall which is visited monthly by the Scottish National Orchestra. Also in City Square is the Tourist Information Office (Telephone 27723). With matching pillars at the other end of Reform Street is Dundee High School and, beyond, the shoulder of Dundee Law, worth climbing for the view.

Continue along High Street, cross it, and leave what local people call 'the Triangle' on your right. To the left, then, along Commercial Street, is the Museum and Art Gallery. Ahead is Murraygate, now pedestrianised, thronged at midday and deserted in the evening. At the far end is the modern Wellgate Centre, a shopping precinct which also contains the city's Central Library.

For this first glimpse, however, go a few paces to your right, along the second side of 'the Triangle'. Opposite you will be the Cathedral Church of St Paul, in Communion with the Church of England and principal church of the See of Brechin. To your left Seagate – so called because the sea once reached this far – two centuries Dundee has been creeping out into the Tay (please read the Dundonian '... gate' as '... gait', i.e. a place where you can walk).

Go ahead down Commercial Street and turn left to the footbridge. Cross it to the Custom House, beside which is the modern harbour (we lost the old one when the Tay Road Bridge was built), accommodating the *Unicorn*, believed to be the oldest wooden battleship still afloat.

Try now picking your way back along the waterfront to the station. What a mess when a city tries too obsequiously to 'come to terms' with the motor car.

DUNDEE–ABERDEEN
by Cahill Kerr

The service from Dundee to Aberdeen is roughly hourly in each direction and consists of the Aberdeen to Glasgow and Edinburgh ScotRail expresses as well as the Inter-City 125 trains to London King's Cross. Passenger accommodation is, therefore, usually of the most modern type and all trains have buffet facilities. The journey time varies from about one hour and ten minutes to one hour and twenty-five minutes. There are station buffets at Aberdeen and Dundee, and general passenger facilities at the intermediate stations are quite adequate. All stations are well placed for the town centres with the exception of Stonehaven, where it may be desirable to take a bus into town.

Dundee Tay Bridge Station is left through the fairly lengthy Dock Street Tunnel and as the train climbs into the daylight the site of the former Dundee East Station is on the left, although no trace of it remains today. On the riverside are many battered industrial complexes that serve as a stark reminder of the city's unemployment problem. Across the Tay Estuary are the Fife towns of Newport and Tayport. Before the opening of the first Tay Bridge in 1878 a journey from Edinburgh to Dundee would have involved a ferry crossing from Tayport to Broughty Ferry, which is the first of the six intermediate stations that are served by local trains between Dundee and Arbroath. This stretch of line was opened in 1838 and was originally built to a gauge of 5 feet 6 inches; indeed two of the other railways in this area, the Dundee & Newtyle, and the Arbroath & Forfar were constructed with gauges of 4 feet 6 inches and 5 feet 6 inches respectively. Farther up the coast one needs to watch the windows and listen for shouts of 'fore' because golf is definitely the name of the game! One of these seaside links, at Carnoustie, used to host the Open Championship. Appropriately, St Andrews, the home of golf, can be glimpsed across the sea on a clear day. Approaching Arbroath look out for Kerr's miniature railway on the right and Gayfield Park, the home of Arbroath Football Club who in 1885 scored a record 36–0 win over Aberdeen Bon Accord in a Scottish Cup match! Arbroath's other claim to fame is the ruined Abbey which in 1320 was the scene of the Declaration of Arbroath asserting Scotland's independence from England.

The present direct line from Arbroath to Montrose was the last part of the route to be completed, opening to passengers as late as 1883. Just out of the station the former trackbed of the Arbroath & Forfar Railway, closed to passengers in 1955, goes off to the left. A few miles farther on the expansive beach at Lunan Bay can be seen, shortly before the train enters a 1½-mile single-track section and descends into Montrose on a sixteen-arch red-brick viaduct. A good panoramic view of Montrose Basin can be had from here, and it is crossed on another bridge just before arrival at the station.

Just outside Montrose the solum of the former Caledonian main line from Perth via Forfar comes into view and joins at Kinnaber, one of the most famous junctions in railway history. This was the 'finishing-post' for the 1895 'race to the North' when the East and West Coast companies were engaged in fierce competition for the fastest London to Aberdeen schedule. The junction was operational until 1981 when British Rail withdrew the remaining freight service from the Brechin branch. The line from Bridge of Dun to Brechin was taken over by the Brechin Railway Preservation Society who are progressing well towards starting a passenger service. (For those interested their address is Brechin Station, 2 Park Road, Brechin, Angus, DD9 7AF.) The station is well worth a look, and a regular bus service runs from Montrose.

The route from Kinnaber to Aberdeen, which was opened in 1850, now heads inland and over the Mearns, an unspectacular yet beautiful area of Scotland. Lewis Grassic Gibbon, author of *Sunset Song*, hailed from these parts. And so to Stonehaven which boasts the best harbour between Arbroath and Aberdeen. The sixteenth-century Tolbooth on the quay houses a local history museum. Near to Stonehaven, down the coast road, are the very impressive ruins of Dunnottar Castle, which is perched on the sea cliffs and at one time sheltered the Crown Jewels of Scotland. The castle can be seen in the distance by looking back over the town as the train leaves Stonehaven.

The spectacular nature of the rocky coastline from here to Aberdeen makes it one of the few high spots of the entire journey from London. There are a few large housing developments to the south of Aberdeen and at Portlethen the station was reopened by British Rail in 1985 in a joint venture with Grampian Regional Council. As the train approaches Aberdeen it sweeps past Nigg Bay and Girdleness Lighthouse, and after passing the freight sidings crosses the River Dee. On the left is Ferryhill engine shed and the junction of the former Deeside line which was closed in 1966. As the guard may say, 'This train will shortly be arriving in Aberdeen station.'

CITY OF ABERDEEN
by Cahill Kerr

Aberdeen is Scotland's third largest city and has much to offer the visitor, both within its boundaries and as a centre for exploring the north-east corner of Scotland.

The University is one of the oldest in Britain and the impressive building of Marischal College, one of the three main University sites, is situated just off the east end of Union Street. Also in the vicinity are the Mercat Cross, the Sheriff Court, and the Tourist Information Centre.

There are three museums and an art gallery in the city. The most outstanding of these is the Maritime Museum in Shiprow, which details the history of fishing, shipbuilding, and the North Sea oil and gas industry. Provost Skene's House is in Guestrow and contains rooms set out in styles ranging from the Cromwellian to the Victorian. James Dun's House in Schoolhill holds an interesting and varied programme of special exhibitions. Diagonally opposite this is the art gallery, with part of Robert Gordon's College next door.

A short bus journey from the city centre will take the visitor to Old Aberdeen. Of interest here is King's College (another part of the University), the Old Town House (now a public library), the Cruickshank Botanic Garden, and St Machar's Cathedral. In the summer months walkabout tours of the area are available. Next to the cathedral is Seaton Park; walking through here it is possible to pick up the River Don and follow it round to the Brig o' Balgownie, round which are some very attractive preserved houses.

In addition to Seaton Park there is also Hazlehead Park to the west of the city which has a wide range of recreational facilities, including a maze and three golf-courses, and Duthie Park to the south with its winter gardens.

For entertainment Aberdeen is fortunate to have two outstanding venues: His Majesty's Theatre was completely renovated and reopened in 1982, and more recently the Music Hall received similar treatment and now hosts a wide range of musical events. It is also worth checking on the programme at the Arts Centre in King Street.

Aberdeen is a good centre for exploring the north-east and Northern Scottish operate an extensive network of bus services into the surrounding area. Of particular interest would be a trip down Royal Deeside to Ballater and Braemar. Also worth while is a run out to the Grampian Transport Museum at Alford. Here there is also a small railway museum, two narrow-gauge railways, and Haughton House Country Park. There are plenty of reasonably priced day tours from Aberdeen, for example, the Castle Trail, the Whisky Trail, and the Fishing Heritage Trail run by Northern Scottish.

ABERDEEN–INVERNESS
by Cahill Kerr

The service between Aberdeen and Inverness consists of eight trains a day in each direction. These are normally made up of older Mark 1 and 2 carriages and most provide a trolley buffet service. The journey takes two hours and twenty-five minutes and despite it being a single line delays are not common. The passenger facilities at the intermediate stations are reasonable, except for Elgin where the building is too small. All are within easy walking distance of the town centres with the possible exception of Keith. There are good Tourist Information Centres at Inverurie, Huntly, Elgin, Forres, and Nairn.

Prior to 1867 trains for the North left the Great North of Scotland Railway (GNSR) terminus at Waterloo Quay, situated along the harbour from the present station and still used today as a small goods depot. Relations between the GNSR and the Southern companies were not good, to the cost of the passengers. The GNSR did not like its trains to be held up by late arrivals from the South at Guild Street, so, instructions were issued that the gates at Waterloo were to be closed when the train was due to depart. Fortunately common sense prevailed and a joint station was opened on the present site in 1867. The name 'joint station' can still occasionally be heard in Aberdeen to this day.

After passing under Union Street the train enters Union Terrace Gardens (Aberdeen's answer to Princes Street Gardens!) where the site of the old turntable is visible on the left. Then it is through two short tunnels and up the hill to Kitty-brewster, the original terminus when the line was opened to Huntly in 1854. The extension down to Waterloo was opened three years later. There are still a number of sidings at Kittybrewster but its glory days as a steam-engine shed are long gone. The train passes through the suburbs of Aberdeen and arrives at Dyce, the former junction for the Buchan lines to Fraserburgh and Peterhead which lost their passenger services in 1965. It is hard to imagine that at one time there were nine stations between here and Aberdeen. These formed part of the suburban service known locally as 'The Subbies' that ran between Dyce and Culter, on the Deeside line, until their withdrawal in 1937. Dyce Station was closed in 1967 but reopened in 1984 with joint funding from British Rail and Grampian Regional Council. Aberdeen Airport, the world's busiest heliport, can be seen on the left.

The line now takes to the countryside and before long the River Don is picked up and stays close by until Inverurie, where it is crossed just before arrival at the station. Between Dyce and Inverurie the line follows closely the course of the former Aberdeen-shire Canal which was bought by the railway. Before the deal was completed the contractor, in his impatience, drained the canal and left all the barges high and dry. Consequently, it had to be refilled to allow them to reach their destinations. Inverurie is the administrative centre of Gordon District and the main town of the area known as 'The Garioch' (pronounced geerie). This is one of the most interesting parts of Britain for archaeological remains. There are thirteen prehistoric sites all within a few miles of the town. On the left of the station is the site of the former GNSR locomotive works. One of the local junior football teams still has the name Inverurie Loco Works. Inverurie was also the junction for the branch to Old Meldrum which closed to passengers in 1931.

Bennachie is now prominently in view; there are five peaks in this range of hills, the highest reaching to 1,733 feet. Here there are extensive forest trails and hill walks, and on top of the Mither Tap O' Bennachie there are considerable remains of a Pictish fort. About 3 miles out of Inverurie are the remnants of Inveramsay Junction where the line to Macduff, closed to passengers in 1951, branched off. At Insch the remains of the medieval Dunnideer Castle can be seen on top of the hill bearing the same name. The 5 miles from Insch to Kennethmont is the only surviving section of double track on the entire line.

The next stop is the attractive town of Huntly which is the centre of the area known as 'Strathbogie'. The River Bogie joins the Deveron at the north end of the town. The main place of interest here is the impressive ruined castle that was completed in 1602. Leaflet guides to the Architectural Trail and walks round Huntly are available at the Tourist Information Centre, which is in the same building as the local museum.

The line was extended from Huntly to Keith in 1856. About 5 miles from Huntly the River Deveron is crossed on a five-skew-arched viaduct. The approach to Keith is heralded by a veritable mountain of empty whisky barrels. Keith was once an important railway centre, where the GNSR met with the Highland Railway (HR). The line on the left-hand side of the platform if the former Great North line to Elgin via Rothes. Until 1985 British Rail ran a limited freight service as far as Dufftown – some 11 miles. This line now plays host to the 'Northern Belle' excursion train run by Grampian Railtours Ltd. The train runs twice weekly in the summer and provides an excellent day out, using First Class carriages with meals served at the tables. At Dufftown there is the chance to see round the Glenfiddich Distillery. (Information about the 'Northern Belle' can be obtained from Grampian Railtours Ltd, Guild Street, Aberdeen.)

The town of Fochabers, about equidistant from Keith and Elgin, is worth a visit and a regular bus service is available from either town. Here there is a folk museum and the famous Baxter's food company has a visitor centre at their factory.

The railway from Aberdeen to Keith and the Dufftown branch is all that remains of the once-extensive GNSR network. The rest of the line to Inverness is over former HR metals. It was opened from Inverness to Nairn in 1855 and on to Keith in 1858. After Keith the train enters a picturesque wooded area and crosses the River Spey, the fastest in Scotland, near Orton. Just beyond the bridge is the former line from Rothes which only enjoyed an eight-year life span. This short branch was closed in 1866, thus making it one of the earliest closures in railway history.

Elgin, the administrative capital of Moray District, is easily the largest intermediate place on the whole route but paradoxically has easily the worst station – one of the original British Rail boxes, but hopefully this situation will be remedied soon. Adjacent to the present station is the impressive structure of the former GNSR station, from where trains used to run to Lossiemouth, the Moray coast, and Speyside. When erected, Elgin Cathedral was regarded as the most beautiful in Scotland and was known as the 'Lantern of the North'. Unfortunately it was burned down in the fourteenth century by the Wolf of Badenoch, although the ruins are most impressive. There are many other interesting buildings in the town including quite a sizeable local museum. The 40-acre Cooper Park provides an excellent range of recreational facilities. Pluscarden Abbey, 6 miles south-west of Elgin houses an active Benedictine community and is open to visitors.

Of interest from an operational point of view is that from Elgin to Inverness the line is still on token working. The freight line to Burghead, which handles grain traffic, can be seen going off to the right about 5 miles out of Elgin. Just before the station at Forres is Mosset park, home of the local Highland League football team Forres Mechanics, who once had a goalkeeper with a wooden leg! Until 1965 Forres was the junction for the original HR main line to Aviemore over Dava Moor. Forres itself is a very old, attractive town and over recent years it has been successful in the British in Bloom competition. There is a museum and a few interesting stones and monuments. A leaflet, *Walks Around Forres*, is available from the Tourist Information Centre. Brodie Castle, which dates mainly from 1645, is situated about 3 miles from the town.

On leaving Forres the train crosses the River Findhorn and makes for Nairn. Nairn is an old spa town and one of the North's most popular seaside resorts. It has also become an internationally known Mecca for golfers. It was once the centre of a thriving fishing community and the old Fishertown, with its museum, provides an insight into former times. About 5 miles south-west of Nairn is Cawdor Castle which

Elgin. (*Photo:* N. Jinkerson)

40

is part of a conservation area with many woodland walks. The castle dates back to the fourteenth century and Cawdor parish church to 1619.

As the train heads towards Inverness, looking across the Moray Firth there is the Black Isle Peninsula, and eventually the Kessock Bridge that connects it with Inverness comes into view. Inverness Airport is situated at Dalcross about 7 miles out of the city. On the approach to Inverness is the junction with the line from Perth and shortly the train runs into the station where it is 'Failte do'n Ghaidhealtachd' or 'Welcome to the Highlands' for those who only speak English!

PERTH–INVERNESS
by Richard Ardern

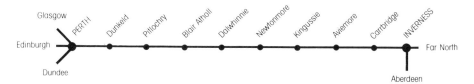

As the train leaves Perth, you will notice on your left some of the industries of the town, principally the whisky industry. On the right-hand side, as we cross the River Almond you will see the wide River Tay, which, among other activities, is famous for its salmon-fishing. Farther to the east lies one of the most historic places in Scotland, Scone, which was once the ancient capital of the Pictish Kingdom. From AD 850 Coronations took place here on the Stone of Destiny, an oblong block of red sandstone, which in 1296, was stolen by Edward I of England and incorporated in the Coronation Chair in Westminster Abbey. The present Palace of Scone, home of the Earl of Mansfield, is visibile through the trees. On the left you will also see the new A9 road. This has now been reconstructed over its whole length from Perth to the Cromarty Firth, some 130 miles, at the cost of £250,000,000.

We are now approaching the village of Stanley. It was formerly a junction: the main line used to go straight on here to Forfar and Aberdeen, but this has now been closed and lifted and Aberdeen traffic goes through Dundee. The area is well known for its soft fruit growing and you may well see fields of raspberry canes. At Stanley the train slows and moves from the double track on to the single track to Inverness on a sweeping bend to the left. On a single-track railway it is necessary to have loops where trains going in opposite directions can cross each other. This may explain the sometimes lengthy station stops.

A mile or so after the village of Murthly we enter Kingswood Tunnel, which is 310 yards long and the first of three tunnels on the line. The line itself was built as far as Dunkeld in 1856; it was then extended through to Inverness in 1863. The line from Dunkeld to Inverness was built by Joseph Mitchell, an Inspector of Roads under Thomas Telford and later a great railway engineer. The 104 miles from Dunkeld to Forres on the original route was built in the remarkable time of twenty-three months.

As we continue downhill towards Dunkeld you will notice on the right-hand side that the hills are beginning to close in. This is because we are about to cross the Highland Boundary Fault, which is represented by this line of hills trending north-east to south-west; and Dunkeld itself could well be called the 'Gateway to the Highlands', as we go through a narrow pass into the first of the many straths that the railway will follow.

Dunkeld Station is actually situated in the village of Birnam across the River Tay from Dunkeld. This village has, of course, been immortalised in Shakespeare's *Macbeth*, in the passage:

Macbeth shall never vanquished be until
Great Birnam Wood to high Dunsinane hill
Shall come against him.

Birnam Hill is actually to the south of the village and was once covered by a Royal Forest. Dunsinane hill is 8 miles north-east of Perth towards the coast.

Dunkeld is a most attractive town, and the National Trust for Scotland owns twenty restored houses mostly dating from the rebuilding of the town following the Battle of Dunkeld in 1689; the Cathedral dates from 1318.

Leaving Dunkeld Station, we will cross the River Bran and enter Dunkeld Tunnel, which is 350 yards long.

Emerging from the cuttings after the tunnel, we head along the wide strath of the River Tay, which we cross at Dalguise on an iron-girder bridge embellished with castellated stone towers, which were required by the Dukes of Atholl as being more in keeping with the area.

This part of Perthshire owes much to the Dukes of Atholl whose land it is, particularly in the wooded nature of the landscape. Between the years 1738 and 1830 the Dukes succeeded in planting the incredible total of 14,000,000 larch trees plus millions of other trees of all kinds.

We are now approaching Ballinluig, where the River Tay parts company with us, swinging its way to the west and running through Aberfeldy (with its famous Wade Bridge) and Kenmore to Loch Tay. We begin to follow the River Tummel. On the left you will notice the bridge that used to carry the Aberfeldy Branch Railway, which was closed in 1965, just three months short of its centenary.

We are now nearing Pitlochry. It is a town of nearly 3,000 inhabitants and is a favourite tourist centre. It has an eighteen-hole golf-course of championship standard, and the Highland Games are held here on the second Saturday in September. It has literary associations in that Robert Louis Stevenson wrote *'Thrawn Janet'* and other short stories here. It is also famous for its festival theatre, which was recently rehoused in an attractive new building on the west side of the river with an auditorium seating 540 people. One of the routes to the theatre is across the dam created by the North of Scotland Hydro-electric Board. This holds back Loch Faskally, a most attractive artificial loch. The Tummel Valley Hydro Scheme extends over a wide area as far north as Dalwhinnie and tunnels channel water from Lochs Ericht and Garry to Lochs Rannoch, Tummel, and Faskally through eight power-stations with the capacity of 245 megawatts and an average annual output of 653,000,000 units. One consequence of the diversion of water for the hydro-electric schemes is that the rivers we follow to the north between here and Dalwhinnie will be noticeably depleted of water. As we approach the town you will see on the right the huge Atholl Palace Hotel and on the left a distillery – yet another example of the diverse activities that go on in Pitlochry.

Leaving Pitlochry, we now see the waters of Loch Faskally on the left. In a little while we will cross under the road bridge that is the start of the old Road to the Isles 'by Tummel and Loch Rannoch'. A few miles along this road is the Queen's View of Loch Tummel, much praised by Queen Victoria, hence the name. We then enter the Pass of Killiecrankie, a spectacular gorge in the River Garry, beyond the north end of which is the site of the Battle of Killiecrankie, fought in 1689 when the forces of William and Mary were routed by those of the exiled King James VII of Scotland (King James II of England), under Bonnie Dundee. One of the routed soldiers is said to have leapt across the gorge, a distance of 17 feet, at a point now known as the 'Soldier's Leap'. This is the farthest point visible on the left-hand side before we enter the 128-yard long Killiecrankie Tunnel.

Entering Blair Atholl, we cross another castellated bridge, and on the left you will see a working water-wheel where the mill has been restored as a museum. Blair Castle is the seat of George Murray, the tenth Duke of Atholl, the only man in Britain to have his own private army, the Atholl Highlanders. The castle is open to visitors and will be glimpsed on the right just after we leave the station. The oldest parts date from the twelfth century but the castle was extensively restored in the nineteenth century.

Blair Atholl used to be a very busy railway centre. There was an engine shed, which you will see on the left after the station, and it was the point where steam trains used to take on a banker to help them up the fearsome gradients to Drumochter Summit, which is the highest main-line railway summit in Britain. The line rises from 450 to 1,484 feet, and the length of hill with the ruling gradient between 1:80 and 1:70 for 18 miles meant that long delays were being experienced with heavy goods trains travelling upwards. About the turn of the century the decision was taken to double the line between Blair Atholl and Dalwhinnie. This decision paid off handsomely in both world wars when the Highland Railway was called upon to carry a very heavy traffic to the naval ports in the north such as Invergordon and Scapa Flow. With the downturn in traffic on the railway the section was singled again in 1966 but with the advent of the off-shore oil industry it has been redoubled in the 1970s.

You will see the hamlet of Bruar on the left-hand side with the Clan Donnachaidh Museum (this is the Robertson clan), and on the right-hand side are the most spectacular Bruar Falls.

We are now approaching Dalnacardoch, and immediately after the old signal-box on the right we will cross under General Wade's Military Road that ran from Stirling and Crieff to Inverness and was built in the 1720s. This crosses the Garry on the right of the original Wade Bridge. You will notice that the Garry, which we have been following, is a mere trickle of water in a rather large watercourse; this is because its headwaters have been diverted for hydro-electric purposes. For the next 15 miles red deer can frequently be seen feeding either beside the track or higher up the hills.

Dalnaspidal has a place in the record books as the highest main-line station in Britain at about 1,400 feet. On the left you will see Loch Garry, the waters of which are transferred by tunnel north-westwards to Loch Ericht *en route* south to the Rannoch power-station.

Two miles farther on we come to Drumochter – the name means 'upper ridge'. The summit is preceded on the right by the ruined County March railway cottages, the summit itself having blue name boards on either side proclaiming the fact that it is 1,484 feet above sea-level. This point is also the boundary between Tayside and Highland Regions. In winter the road is frequently blocked here by snow but the trains almost invariably get through. In the worst weather the line is patrolled regularly by a locomotive with snow-plough.

The hills on either side of us reach 3,000 feet. But on the descent to Newtonmore following the River Truim, you will see much hummocky terrain. These are moraines of sands and gravels left behind from the last glaciation. In places you can also see flat terraces where these gravels have been reworked by rivers that have subsequently cut down deeper into their own flood plains.

At Dalwhinnie, which is 1,174 feet above sea-level, we see Loch Ericht on the left-hand side beyond the dam. This loch is 16 miles long and forms a major part of the Tummel Hydro Scheme, which centres on Pitlochry. Dalwhinnie was formerly an important stopping-place for travellers by road but is quieter now that it has been bypassed by the new A9. On the right past the station (which is now an unstaffed halt) is a malt-whisky distillery with its distinctive pagoda roof.

The section from Dalwhinnie follows the River Truim until it joins the Spey which comes in from the west, having its headwaters up in the Corrieyairack Pass, which is traversed by another military road ascending to 2,500 feet on the way over to Fort Augustus and the southern end of Loch Ness.

Newtonmore is the home of the Clan MacPherson Museum, which was established just after the war. The staff at Newtonmore Station have won many prizes for the station garden. Newtonmore is less than 30 miles from the West Highland Railway at Tulloch; but though a rail link between the two has never been built, the road linking them was traversed by the last stage-coach in Britain until 1914.

Kingussie, pronounced with the 'g' silent, is a larger town than Newtonmore with a population of 1,100 and was founded in the late eighteenth century by the Duke of Gordon as a wool town. It has a secondary school, and new industries in the station yard on the left include the manufacture of bone china and precision tools. The Highland Folk Museum is an important tourist attraction based partly on the Scandinavian model of open-air museums. A reconstructed thatched black house will be seen on the left as we leave the station. On the right will be seen Ruthven Barracks about a mile away perched on a mound. This extensive ruin was built by the Government in 1718 and burned by the Highlanders who re-formed here in 1746 after the Battle of Culloden.

On the right you will observe that we have been following the Spey Marshes, an important resource for wildlife. In winter the area can be completely flooded on both sides of the railway. Part of the marshes have been designated as a Nature Reserve and drain into Loch Insh, which is used for sailing and canoeing.

After Kincraig we can see ahead on the right the Duke of Gordon's Monument; the granite column is 90 feet high situated on top of Tore Alvie, which itself reaches a height of 1,175 feet; near it is the Waterloo Cairn in memory of the Gordon Highlanders who fell in that battle. Abreast of the monument we pass Loch Alvie on the left-hand side.

We are now approaching Aviemore, which is a major all-the-year-round tourist centre known particularly for the skiing on the western slopes of the Cairngorms. From a railway town Aviemore has expanded rapidly since 1960 and now has a population of 1,500. The Aviemore Centre comprises a collection of hotels and entertainments such as an ice-rink, swimming-pool, and dry ski slope. Apart from skiing and climbing, other attractions of the area include Britain's only reindeer herd high up on the Cairngorms, sailing on Loch Morlich, and various nature walks.

Aviemore Station was much enlarged in 1892 just before the direct line to Inverness was opened. The route was previously 26 miles longer travelling through Grantown, Forres, and Nairn to reach Inverness from a north-easterly direction. The first 5 miles of the old route are now owned by the Strathspey Railway Company, whose turntable and station can be seen on the right on leaving the station. Also visible will be some of their locomotives and rolling-stock outside the original engine shed.

The views of the Cairngorms on a clear day are superb, and you can see the deep defile of the Lairig Ghru, a pass that goes right through to Deeside in Aberdeenshire. To the left of it is Cairngorm, standing 4,084 feet high with the ski developments running up towards it; and to the right of Lairig Chru is Braeriach, some 4,248 feet high.

Carrbridge was for five years the terminus of the direct line to Inverness. It is a holiday village with hotels, a ski school, and the well-known Landmark Visitor Centre. This, though not visible from the train, has a multi-screen auditorium, exhibition, bookshop, and restaurant. There are wildlife trails, including one at tree-top level, and a sculpture park. An audio-visual show about the Highlands is screened frequently throughout the day.

From Carrbridge we cross the River Dulnain, and start the steepest part of the climb at 1:60 up towards Slochd summit, climbing from 900 to 1,315 feet. The next bridge we cross is over the Baddengorm Burn, the scene of a freak accident in 1914 when water from a cloudburts was ponded back behind fallen trees and debris and broke through, hitting the bridge just as a train was crossing; one coach fell into the stream and five lives were lost. The power of the water can be seen from the size of the boulders in the stream-bed on the left, but the massive size of the reconstructed bridge in relation to the small size of the stream provides reassurance to present-day travellers.

The line curves round from a westerly direction to head northwards, passing on the right the huge glacial meltwater channel known as the 'Slochd Mor' or 'big trench' but now partly filled in by the new A9. A final rock cutting takes the railway up to the summit at Slochd, which is 1,315 feet above sea-level, a fact that is marked by a name board on the left. A passing loop here has been reinstated and is controlled from Aviemore signal-box; but in steam days this was the point where banking or pilot engines from either direction would have been detached from the trains to run back to Inverness or Aviemore.

The view opening up on the left is of Strathdearn with the River Findhorn heading south-westwards towards its headwaters. We will shortly be crossing the river on the Tomatin Viaduct, a curving structure with nine spans standing 143 feet above the river. Tomatin, like Dalwhinnie, is a distillery village but the distillery is of much more recent origin and does not have the old-style pagoda-type building that you saw at Dalwhinnie. The malt distillery here is, however, the largest in Scotland with over twenty stills and is now owned by Japanese business interests.

Just after Tomatin you will see on the left some tree-stumps buried in the peat. This is quite a common occurrence throughout the Highlands and shows that the area was much more heavily wooded in times past. The climate has changed and some of these areas are now above the tree-line but in many areas the trees would re-establish themselves if the ground was not grazed by sheep and deer.

Looking out on the right, we get a good view of the Findhorn Valley with a wide flood plain before, in the distance, the river heads into the narrow gorge known as the 'Streens'.

Approaching Moy, we see on the right Loch Moy with a monument on the islands marking the burial-place of the Clan MacKintoch, whose present Chief lives in Moy Hall, which may just be glimpsed at the far end of the loch.

Approaching Daviot, we begin to see more extensive views on a clear day. We are now into the valley of the River Nairn and get a good view towards the south-west upstream. Across the valley is Daviot village with its white church built to a design by Thomas Telford in the early nineteenth century. We are again on a 1:60 gradient, and trains coming out of Inverness had a hard struggle in steam days starting from cold. Because of this, the section from Daviot to Culloden Moor used to be double track; and it is the only bit on the line that has not been reinstated after being torn up in the 1960s. The line is now trending north-eastwards away from Inverness owing to the need to keep the gradient within the capabilities of heavily loaded trains.

Inverness lies on the other side of the ridge across the valley on the left. On a clear day the distant Ben Wyvis can be seen dominating the horizon. The ridge itself is the well-known Drumossie Moor on which in 1746 was fought the last battle on British soil, the Battle of Culloden. The Highland troops of Prince Charles Edward Stuart were defeated by the forces of George II under the Duke of Cumberland. The battlefield is now owned by the National Trust for Scotland who are busy restoring it from its present wooded state to open moorland over which the battle was fought. The Trust have a visitor centre on the site, which can easily be reached by bus from Inverness, and which is one of the main tourist attractions of the area. A visit to the battlefield may be combined with the walk of about a mile to the prehistoric Clava Cairns, which are down on the valley bottom hidden within a stand of trees just before the viaduct. Visible ahead on the left is the Culloden Viaduct, a huge structure with twenty-nine arches crossing a distance of 600 yards and 128 feet above the river; the middle arch has a span of 100 feet and the other spans are each 50 feet. The scale of the viaduct is, however, best appreciated from ground-level.

The line is now changing direction and soon we will be heading westwards down the final slope to Inverness. The line descends partly through forest but there are glimpses from time to time of the Moray Firth, and one can see across the water the villages of Avoch (pronounced och) and Fortrose together with the peninsula known as the Black Isle trending north-eastwards. On a clear day one can pick out the conical peak of Sgurr a'Mhuillin, which is almost as far west as Achnasheen; but the dominant mountain in this scene is the great mass of Ben Wyvis, which rises to a height of 3,400 feet.

Inverness has earned its title as 'Capital of the Highlands'. With a population of 42,000 it is the largest town in the Highlands and Islands, and the centre for communications and administration. It boasts a modern theatre, Eden Court, on the banks of the River Ness and a variety of activities are staged throughout the summer months for the benefit of visitors. It makes an ideal centre for touring the North of Scotland, and you may travel by train to places such as Kyle of Lochalsh opposite the Isle of Skye on the west coast, to Wick or Thurso on the north coast, or eastwards to Aberdeen.

INVERNESS–WICK/THURSO
by Leslie Turner

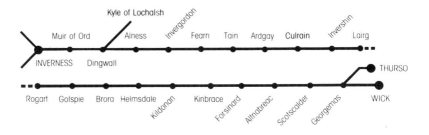

Viewed from the south, Inverness is often seen as the north of Scotland; but it is by no means the end of the rail network, for Wick, in Caithness, is 161 rail miles farther north. Inverness is the limit for through trains from London, but three daily trains run from here to Wick and Thurso each weekday, with one as far as Lairg only on Sundays.

Shortly after leaving Inverness Station, we cross the viaduct over the River Ness and then slow to walking pace to cross a swing bridge over the Caledonian Canal, the waterway built by Thomas Telford early in the nineteenth century. The train then speeds along the shores of the Beauly Firth, through a landscape of barley and yellow fields of oilseed rape. The line turns north at the head of the Firth, past Beauly village, whose station is closed; but soon after a stop is made at Muir of Ord, where the station was also closed, but then reopened in 1976. Here there is also a grain silo where barley is brought by rail to supply local distillers.

The line drops to cross the River Conon, which flows into the Cromarty Firth, and shortly we arrive at Dingwall, the old county town of Ross and Cromarty. The town of some 4,000 people nestles at the foot of Ben Wyvis, and just north of the station the rail line to Kyle of Lochalsh strikes off to the west.

The line is now operated by radio signalling from a Portacabin on Dingwall Station platform. By this method, significant savings in staff have been made and the once-familiar semaphore signals have disappeared.

Our train follows the shore of the Cromarty Firth – with Black Isle across the water. This is not quite an island, being joined to the 'mainland' between Muir of Ord and Conon Bridge. The new causeway of the A9 road sweeps across the Firth and up over the Black Isle and thence via the new Kessock Bridge to Inverness.

High on the hill to the west can be seen a monument built centuries ago by a landowner to create work for unemployed masons. Between Evanton (24 miles from Inverness) and Invergordon the scenery becomes more industrial, the Firth being full of oil-rigs in for repair – or currently mothballed owing to the fall in oil prices. At Alness, the previously closed station was reopened in 1973. At Invergordon, the many oil-tanks are a reminder of the port's history as the base of the Royal Navy Home Fleet until 1939. The harbour here has over 40 feet of water at low tide. We then pass Invergordon Distillers' plant, which makes grain spirit from wheat or maize as a base for blended whisky, gin, and vodka. To the left are the remains of the huge aluminium-smelter which closed with the loss of 800 jobs in 1981.

Across the water can be seen the gap between headlands, The Soutar, which leads to the North Sea. On the left is an oil-rig construction yard and on the right the village of Cromarty which is a charming spot well worth a visit. It has many fine houses of the Georgian period which reflect its past importance as a major port and manufacturing centre.

The line now passes through rich agricultural land noted for its seed-potato pro-duction to reach the Dornoch Firth near Tain. This estuary is the last one on Britain's eastern coastline with no industrial development, though the peace is disturbed by jet planes which come here from the South of England and Germany to practise at bombing ranges.

Beyond Tain, a small town with a population of 2,000, the line runs alongside the Dornoch Firth – but the Railway Development Society and a number of other bodies would like to see it cross the Firth on a new bridge and serve the town of Dornoch before rejoining the existing route at Golspie.

This is not just wishful thinking. Some £300,000,000 of public money is currently being spent on works to improve the A9 trunk road to Wick, including a £20,000,000 bridge across the Dornoch Firth. These measures will make the road journey to the far north considerably shorter than the rail journey. ScotRail has taken seriously the idea of a rail track as well as a road across this proposed bridge, and Chris Green, its then General Manager, said in July 1985, 'If the major opportunity of the rail bridge was missed, an hour's difference between road and rail times could prove catastrophic for the line's future.'

To provide a rail crossing of the Firth would cost some £12,700,000 – a small sum in comparison to that being spent on the road. Besides, more than half of this amount could be found by the Highlands and Islands Development Board and other bodies.

A feasibility study prepared for ScotRail for a similar rail bridge revealed that the Far North line stood to lose 25 per cent of its business by competition from the new road in 1990 and this could result in closure of the entire 168-mile line. A new rail bridge, on the other hand, would reduce track mileage and save £375,000 a year in operating costs. The line's £1,000,000 subsidy would be reduced and the Government's

£4,500,000 contribution for the bridge repaid in twelve years.

At the time of writing, the case for Dornoch rail crossing is still being put energetically by the RDS. Fuller details are contained in the Society's pamphlet *The Dornoch Bridge Saga*, available at 60p from 48 The Park, Great Bookham, Leatherhead, Surrey, KT23 3LS.

A consequence of the building of this new rail link could be the abandoning of the Lairg – Golspie section, with Lairg situated at the end of a branch from Tain. It is that route which our train now follows, making a big loop inland. That route was chosen to open up the interior 120 years ago when the line was built.

Past Ardgay, the line keeps to the south of the River Oykel and the Kyles of Sutherland until reaching Culrain at Carbisdale Castle, which is now a youth hostel. The line then climbs rapidly through rocky cuttings to Lairg, a village of some 600 people. The oil depot by the station supplies the ports of Lochinver and Kinlochbervie, which are now among the most important fishing ports in Britain. The railway then turns east, reaching a summit of 488 feet, then dropping down Strath Fleet to the coast and the large village of Golspie with a population of 1,300.

Outside Golspie is the magnificent Dunrobin Castle, home of the Dukes of Sutherland. It was they who were responsible for financing the construction of long stretches

Wick harbour. (*Photo:* E. West)

48

of this line to Caithness in the 1860s. The first Duke acquired the Sutherland estates through marriage, but in his own right was one of the wealthiest men in Britain.

The Duke decided to use resources from his English estates at Trentham Staffordshire, to open up and modernise the North, and many new factories and agricultural improvements were introduced. Great cruelty, however, was inflicted on the local population, who lived at a subsistence level on land which proved more profitable as sheep grazings. Many were evicted from their cottages and shipped to North America. The empty lands of the Highlands are in part a reflection of these evictions, which continued until the 1880s. Subsequent waves of emigration in search of a better life continued the emptying of the countryside.

Brora, 6 miles up the coast from Golspie, shows its industrial past by way of brick-built houses, most uncommon in Scotland. The town used to have a coal-mine and a brickworks. A distillery and a woollen-mill still exist.

We follow the shore, and it is possible to see the Moray coast. The Beatrice oilfield lies a dozen miles offshore north of Helmsdale, and the production platform can just be seen on clear days.

Helmsdale was planned as a village for families cleared from the interior to take up the new trade of fishing. There is now a small crab-processing factory here. Helmsdale owes much of its form to the Duke of Sutherland, one of the streets being Stafford Street.

The line leaves the main road, which follows the coastline, and strikes out again for the interior, following the River Helmsdale, noted for its salmon. Ten miles up the valley at Kildonan, gold was found in 1868, which led to a mini-rush of prospectors. The country becomes bleaker and more rugged as the line slowly climbs. Forsinard is a last outpost of habitation before the train strikes across one of the most isolated parts of Britain. Four miles beyond Forsinard is the summit of the line at 708 feet.

Altanbreac is located in the middle of an area known as the 'Flows' – a unique landscape of peat and water. There is currently a great dispute between those who wish to conserve the area for its wildlife and the foresters who claim that planting trees will bring much-needed jobs to the area. An experimental peat-burning powerstation was built here in the 1950s, and peat is still harvested on the edge of the moor for domestic use and for export to Scandinavia.

At Georgemas Junction, the train splits, with one portion running north to Thurso and the other eastwards to Wick. The flatness of Caithness comes as a surprise to the visitor used to the mountainous west of Scotland. This county is noted for its beef cattle.

Wick is the county town and has a population of 8,000, but is now somewhat overshadowed by Thurso. The town owed its prosperity to the herring fishery and associated fish processing, of which very little remains.

Thurso owes its rapid growth to the establishment of a nuclear research centre at Dounreay, ten miles west of the town, and the development of the car ferry to the Orkney Isles with the additional trade this brings. The town's population has nearly trebled to 9,000 in the last thirty years. We are now more than 700 rail miles from London and at the northernmost limit of the British Rail network.

DINGWALL–KYLE OF LOCHALSH

by Alistair Streeton

The railway journey from Dingwall to Kyle of Lochalsh is one that everyone should experience once in a lifetime. Whatever the time of year – be it summer when the moors are covered with purple heather, or winter when they are blanketed with deep snow – this line is, in my opinion, the most spectacular of them all.

Although most travellers will start their journey at Inverness on one of the three daily trains serving this route, the 63½-mile Kyle line does not begin until you leave Dingwall, a market town with just over 3,800 inhabitants and the administrative headquarters of Ross and Cromarty District. At the station here you can still see the remains of the livestock pens that used to hold sheep and cattle taken by rail from Kyle and the far north.

As our train climbs slowly up the 1:50 incline to Raven Rock, you will discern in the distance the spa village of Strathpeffer, which once boasted a branch line of its own. Nearing the summit you cannot help but observing the dramatic contrast between highlands and lowlands as we enter the Highlands proper.

After leaving Garve, where you can take a bus to the small west coast fishing port of Ullapool, we pass several hydroelectric dams and generating stations. You may be lucky enough to see a salmon leap in the purpose-built fish-ladders on their way to their spawning grounds.

We proceed at a leisurely pace towards Achnasheen, a bleak and lonely place, where north- and south-bound trains pass each other, and where, if one of them is late, you may stretch your legs and maybe take some photographs. Along this section of our route, between Loch Scaven and Loch Gowan we cross the watershed at a height of 634 feet above sea-level. Here those with a keen eye will readily spot the abundant wildlife, particularly deer and birds of many species including the occasional eagle. Indeed, amid so desolate a landscape it is easy to imagine that if you were only to listen intently enough you could hear the cries of wolves.

Approaching Achnashellach Station, we journey through some of the world's oldest rocks – rocks to which clung remnants of primeval Caledonian forest that heath fires were unable to reach and destroy.

Our train then heads towards Strathcarron where we meet the waters of the Atlantic as we skirt the southern shores of Loch Carron with its numerous rocky inlets. Here the magical interplay of light and shadow upon the sea, small islands, cliffs, and mountains that together make up the landscape cannot fail to cast a spell on the onlooker, be the season and the weather what they may. And it is these qualities that have endeared this section of the line to so many photographers over the years.

The railway originally ended at Stromeferry, our next stop; it was not extended to Kyle until 1897, twenty-seven years later. This latter 10¼-mile section was the

Opposite: The ferry from Kyleakin, Skye, arriving at Kyle of Lochalsh. (*Photo:* Roy J. Westlake)

hardest to build, much of it having to be blasted out of solid rock; and, at a cost of £20,000 a mile, it was also the most expensive piece of railway engineering undertaken up till then.

As our train makes its tortuous way to Kyle, you may sense that something has been missing – something you cannot quite put your finger on. And suddenly you realise: no signals! Traffic on the Kyle line is controlled by radio from the signalling centre located at Dingwall. This method of regulating trains has proved highly successful and has reduced the line's operating costs, thus making its future more secure.

Drawing near to Kyle, we can see the breath-taking Cuillin Mountains on the Isle of Skye – often known as the 'Misty Isle' – and, in the distance, the beautiful island of Raasay. Both of these islands can be easily reached and are well worth exploring. There are frequent ferry crossings from Kyle to Skye between 6 a.m. and 11 p.m.; but less frequent crossings from Sconser (on the Isle of Skye) to Raasay. Bus services in this sparsely populated region are basic but adequate – though they may not always connect with trains. Why not explore these islands, then return using the ferry from Armadale to Mallaig across the Sound of Sleat, and the West Highland line to Fort William and Glasgow?

Kyle of Lochalsh itself is a village of some 700 souls and a useful place to stop for one or more nights – perhaps in the forty-five-bedroom Lochalsh Hotel, formerly owned by the railway.

I said at the outset that this is a trip of a lifetime: but, after you have alighted from the train at Kyle, smelt the tang in the air, heard the cry of the gulls and the distant hoot of the ferry, you will, I have no doubt, want to savour this journey again.

Let me conclude with an anecdote I heard a long time ago. As you may notice, the buffers at Kyle are located not far from the pier edge. A tourist about to board the Kyle train at Dingwall went up to the guard and, in a loud piping voice, asked, 'Does this train stop at Kyle, my good man?' 'I hope so, madam,' he fervently replied.

GLASGOW–FORT WILLIAM–MALLAIG–OBAN
by Lewis Buckingham

The West Highland lines from Glasgow to Oban, Fort William, and Mallaig offer the traveller more than just a railway journey. They are a dramatic and unforgettable experience, passing as they do through scenery of breath-taking and unparalleled beauty; and, whether one starts the journey on the overnight Fort William sleeper at London Euston or on one of the thrice-daily trains at Glasgow Queen Street, a sense of adventure prevails. The line has rightly been described as 'the line for all seasons'.

Glasgow–Fort William

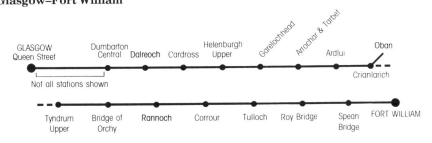

Our journey commences from Glasgow's Queen Street Station and the first 23 miles of the route to Craigendoran follows the River Clyde through Cowlairs, Maryhill, and Westerton where the Glasgow North electric line is joined. On through Drumchapel, Singer, Dalmuir, Kilpatrick, and Bowling where the Clyde Estuary open up before us, and so to the first stop at the shipbuilding town of Dumbarton. The train crosses the River Leven and continues along the banks of the Clyde, where, at Cardross, one can see Port Glasgow on the opposite side of the river. The industrial town of Greenock with its extensive docks lying on the southern shore of the Clyde can be seen from the train at Craigendoran. Here we leave the electric commuter lines and swing away to the right on to the West Highland line proper, having before us the hundred or so miles to Fort William, on a route opened in 1894.

Along the gradually broadening river one has splendid views of the Firth until our next stop at Helensburgh Upper. Helensburgh is a pleasant resort town located in a sheltered position on the shores of the Firth. It was founded in 1776 by Sir James Colquhoun of Luss who named it after his wife.

Horseshoe curve between Tyndrum and Bridge of Orchy. (*Photo:* Chris Burton)

Helensburgh marks the turning-point of our journey: behind us lies the industrialised central belt, before us a continuous vista of mountains, moors, lochs, rivers, and streams.

We follow the edge of Gare Loch to Garelochhead Station; and then, as the mouth of Loch Goil comes into sight from the west, climb high along the side of Loch Long, passing Glen Douglas on the east and Ben Arthur, also known as 'The Cobbler' (2,891 feet), on the west, until we reach Arrocher and Tarbet Station. This is an area popular with tourists, especially those who enjoy walking and climbing. The station is situated in the middle of a narrow neck of land separating Loch Long at Arrochar from Loch Lomond, affording magnificent views of the fabled loch and of Ben Lomond (3,194 feet). At the northern tip of the loch we come to Ardlui, our next stop.

Climbing again, our train continues through beautiful Glen Falloch and the hills of West Perthshire, with the Falls of Falloch on the east, to Crianlarich, a lovely village in an ideal position for touring the Western Highlands. At Crianlarich we are surrounded by mountains with Ben More (3,843 feet) to the east and Ben Oss (3,374 feet), Ben Dhu Craig (3,024 feet), and Ben Lui (3,708 feet) to the west. It is here that the Oban and Fort William lines diverge from one another. Both follow Strath Fillan for about 5 miles a short distance from each other until at Tyndrum they part company, the Oban line swinging westwards, the Fort William line continuing northwards and entering Argyllshire.

Running round the side of Ben Odhar (2,943 feet), we approach the unique Horse Shoe Curve. Crossing a viaduct at the foot of Beinn A Chaistel and another at the foot of the cone-shaped Ben Doran (3,524 feet), the train doubles back on itself to form a horseshoe.

The next stop is at Bridge of Orchy, situated on the south side of lovely Loch Tulla, and an ideal place for exploring the surrounding Highlands. After following the River

No. 37184 on Rannoch Moor with the Fort William–Glasgow and Euston train. (*Photo:* Chris Burton)

Orchy to its source at Loch Tulla, the line strikes out into Perthshire once more and heads towards Rannoch Moor, a wilderness of 20 square miles of peatbogs, tarns, tiny lochs, and streams. Robert Louis Stevenson, perceiving the moor through the eyes of David Balfour, the hero of his novel *Kidnapped*, wrote of it: 'a wearier looking desert man never saw.'

The crossing of this vast area was achieved by 'floating' the line on a mattress of tree roots, larch saplings, and thousands of tons of earth and ash. The train crosses the moor with a view of Loch Laidon on the left, stopping at Rannoch Station, then, with Ben Alder to the east and Stob Na Cruaich to the west, it continues to Corrour on the edge of the moor. Just before Corrour Station it passes through the snowshed over Cruach cutting which protects the cutting from snowdrifts on this windswept part of the moor. So beautiful is the desolate landscape that one is continually looking from one side of the carriage to the other for fear of missing any of it.

To the east of Corrour lies Loch Ossian. Appearing to the west just beyond the station are Loch Trieg and Stob Coire Easain (3,658 feet) – the latter dominating the hills that rise steeply from the shores of the loch – while to the east is Chris Dearg (3,433 feet).

After halting at Tulloch Station, the train wends its way westwards through the Braes of Lochaber and the Monessie Gorge to Roy Bridge at the mouth of Glen Roy. Just past the station on the left is Keppoch House, the ancient seat of the MacDonalds.

The next stop is Spean Bridge, the surrounding area was used during the Second World War as a training ground for Commandos, in commemoration of whom stands a monument on a hill to the right, beyond the station.

The last lap of the journey takes us past the Lochaber Mountains to Fort William, which lies sheltered at the foot of mighty Ben Nevis (4,406 feet), Britain's highest mountain.

Fort William, with a population of 4,200, makes an ideal centre from which to tour the Western Highlands, and the new station complex opened in 1975 embraces both rail and bus services, together with the Tourist Information Office. The West Highland Museum is well worth a visit, and the town has many interesting shops along its main street. A good choice of hotel and guest-house accommodation is available.

Fort William–Mallaig

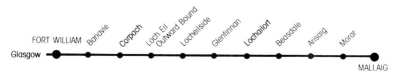

Opened in 1901, the 41¾-mile-long line from Fort William to Mallaig is probably the most scenic in Britain. It carries four trains in each direction a day and in summer some of them are equipped with an observation saloon in which, on payment of a supplementary fare, one may travel and listen to a commentary by a courier explaining and enlarging upon various features of the route. Moreover, ScotRail have recently reintroduced steam locomotives during the tourist season. These added attractions have proved very popular with visitors and have generated additional revenue, thus helping to assure the line's future.

After leaving Fort William, our train parts company with the main line at Mallaig Junction, crosses the River Lochy and, with the towering mass of the Ben Nevis mountain range in the background, continues northwest for about a mile to Banavie, where, after a brief stop, it crosses the swing bridge over the Caledonian Canal. Here, on the right, we can see 'Neptune's Staircase' – a series of locks giving vessels access to the higher reaches of the 60½-mile-long canal, which runs through the Great Glen from Fort William to Inverness.

From Banavie we veer to the west and, about a mile farther on, come to Corpach. It was the establishment of a pulp-paper plant here in the mid 1960s that induced British Rail to retain the West Highland line, which has been used ever since to deliver locally grown timber to the mill and collect finished products from it.

Our train now coasts along the northern shore of Loch Eil, stopping at Loch Eil Outward Bound before reaching Locheilside situated towards the western end of the loch. Meanwhile, Ben Nevis continues to dominate the scene to the east.

Beyond Loch Eil the mountains close in as our train enters a narrow glen from which it emerges 2 miles farther on at Glenfinnan. Then, after making a short detour to the north, it crosses Glenfinnan Viaduct, a graceful concrete structure comprising twenty-one arches rising up to a 100 feet above the ground, and curving in a crescent 1,248 feet across the Finnan Valley. The building of the viaduct was the subject of controversy among contemporaries; its opponents, echoing Wordsworth's sentiments expressed a few decades earlier about the railway's encroachment of his beloved Lake land, believed it would irredeemably mar the beauty of the glen. But today many consider that, far from detracting from the scene, the viaduct enhances it; and it has been compared to a Roman aqueduct.

To the south lies Loch Shiel, at the head of which stands Glenfinnan Monument marking the spot where Charles Edward Stuart, probably better known as Bonnie Prince Charlie, unfurled his standard in 1745. The Visitors' Centre here is well worth a visit and is only a short walk from Glenfinnan Station.

Our route takes us through a narrow wooded glen to the shores of Loch Eilt in which there are numerous islets with tall trees growing on them. From Loch Eilt we follow the River Ailort, which can be seen on the left, until it flows into Loch Ailort. After halting at Lochailort Station, we go through a series of short tunnels, pass the diminutive Loch Dubh on the right, cross Glen Mamie on a viaduct and meet the Atlantic at Loch nan Uamh ('Loch of the Cave'). A further series of tunnels brings us to Arisaig from which we can obtain superb views of the islands of Eigg and Rhum. Eigg may easily be identified by its *scurr* rising to 1,285 feet at the south end, beyond which the peaks of Rhum, a National Nature Reserve, may also be discerned. Cruises to these islands operate from Arisaig.

For the remainder of the journey we head northwards. At Morar, our penultimate stop, we cross a viaduct over the ¼-mile-long River Morar, which flows from Loch Morar. Loch Morar, which can be seen on the right, is the deepest lake in Britain, its extreme depth being 1,017 feet; like Loch Ness, it, too, reputedly contains a monster – here nicknamed 'Morag'! To the west there are enchanting views of the snow-white sands of Morar and, in the distance, the Isle of Skye.

The last 3 miles of our route skirt the rocky coastline. To the east the islands of Eigg and Rhum may still be seen.

Mallaig, the terminus of the 164¼-mile-long West Highland Railway, is a busy small town and fishing port, with some 900 inhabitants. From its pier Caledonian Macbrayne steamers sail to Armadale on the Isle of Skye, and to the small isles of Rhum, Eigg, Muck, and Canna. Mail-boat cruises also operate from here to Loch Nevis, which is accessible only by water. On certain days in the summer it is possible to make a circular tour of Skye; using the steamer service along the Sound of Sleat to Kyle of Lochalsh, the ferry to Kyleakin (on Skye), the coach to Armadale, and the steamer back to Mallaig. Alternatively, those touring Scotland by train might consider making their way to Kyle of Lochalsh by either of these routes and there taking the train to Inverness.

No. 44767 *George Stephenson* approaches Mallaig on *West Highlander*, 1 August 1984. (*Photo:* Chris Burton)

Crianlarich–Oban

Although the Oban and Fort William lines diverge at Crianlarich, they run parallel along Strath Fillan for 5 miles or so as far as Tyndrum, separated from each other only by the river. At Tyndrum, the Oban line branches westwards into Argyllshire and threads its way beside the River Lochy between the hills to Dalmally at the foot of Glen Orchy, which extends some 12 miles north-east to Bridge of Orchy on the Fort William line.

About 1½ miles beyond Dalmally, the ruins of Kilchurn Castle, an ancient stronghold of the Campbell Clan, come into sight as the train swings round the head of Loch Awe. The station at Loch Awe was reopened in 1985, having been closed for twenty years; and from the summer of 1986 it became possible once more to enjoy a cruise on the loch by a small steamer operating from the station pier.

After passing Loch Awe hydro-electric power-station on the right, the train enters the famous Pass of Brander, which connects Loch Awe with Loch Etive. Towering above it to the north stands Ben Cruachan, which, at 3,689 feet, is one of the highest mountains in Argyllshire. Wire fencing protects the railway line below from landslides. We follow the River Awe on the left for about 2 miles before crossing it at Bridge of Awe and continuing for a further 2 miles to Taynuilt, an attractive village situated on the shores of Loch Etive. Today Taynuilt is a resort popular with anglers and with climbers of Ben Cruachan, and from its pier there are occasional cruises of the loch. But until the last century it was the main iron-smelting centre in Scotland, priding itself on supplying cannon and shot for the Royal Navy.

57

On leaving Taynuilt we run along the southern shore of Loch Etive to Connel Ferry where a spectacular cataract known as the 'Falls of Lora' can be seen at the mouth of the loch. The ferry was replaced in 1903 by a large cantilever bridge which used to carry both the road and the railway north to Ballachulish until 1965 when the road across it was widened following the closure of the branch line. From here the train embarks upon the final stage of its 42-mile journey from Crianlarich to Oban, passing through Glencruitten.

Oban enjoys a sheltered position on the shores of the sloping bay overlooking the island of Kerrera. Indeed, the name Oban derives from the Gaelic meaning 'bay' or 'creek'. The town owes its development to the coming of the steamboat and the railway in the nineteenth century, and this led to the growth of a thriving tourist industry; today it is a bustling resort with a resident population of 7,000. The skyline is dominated by McCaig's Folly – an incomplete tower built in 1897 by a local philanthropist to provide work for unemployed masons and to serve as a memorial to his family. From it one may view to advantage the sunsets for which Oban is so famous.

From Oban there is a good choice of ferry sailings to the fascinating islands of the Inner and Outer Hebrides: Mull, Iona, Lismore, Staffa, Colonsay, Coll, and Tiree. Small-boat excursions also run direct to the thirteenth-century Duart Castle and the nineteenth-century Torosay Castle, both of which are on the island of Mull. In summer a narrow-gauge railway operates between Craignure and Torosay, connecting with Caledonian MacBrayne's steamer service from Oban. ScotRail offers combined train-boat coach excursions, using its special touring train.

Evenings of traditional Scottish entertainment are regularly held at the Corran Halls as well as at various hotels and restaurants along the front. There are good bathing beaches at Ganavan Sands to the north of the town. Indeed, it may be safely said that Oban caters for all tastes.

CITY OF GLASGOW
by Bill Russell

In the sixth century St Mungo (or Kentigern) founded a church on a site by the River Clyde. From 1175, when King William the Lion granted a Charter, Glasgow developed its trade, agriculture, and manufacturing industries, helped by the river as a source of power and a means of exporting its goods. Development was rapid during the Industrial Revolution and trade with the USA aided Glasgow's prosperity. It was the first city with a steamboat service: in 1812 Henry Bell's *Comet* carried passengers between Glasgow, Greenock, and Helensburgh. The name 'Glasgow' comes from the Celtic *glas-dhu* meaning 'green place' and, although it is Scotland's largest city, it has many beautiful parks such as Rouken Glen, Linn Park, Queen's Park and Victoria Park with its Fossil Grove, not to mention its renowned football grounds! Many of the city's landmarks can be reached by train – stations are named in parentheses.

Cathedral (High Street)
The cathedral is the most complete medieval cathedral on the Scottish mainland. Its rather austere exterior hides an interesting interior with a fourteenth-century timbered roof and the fifteenth-century stone screen and fan vaulting in the crypt housing the Tomb of St Mungo, Glasgow's patron saint.

Opposite: George Square, Glasgow. (*Photo:* Jarrold)

Provand's Lordship
Across the road from the cathedral is Glasgow's oldest house, dating from about 1471.

University
The University, the second in Scotland, was founded in 1451. Its Gothic-style building is sited on Gilmorehill. The Hunterian Museum is worth a visit.

Glasgow Cross
The Tolbooth steeple with its musical bells dates from the seventeenth century.

Glasgow Green (Bridgeton)
Existed 300 years ago. At the People's Palace there is a fascinating display of Glasgow's history and city life.

No visit to the city would be complete without a visit to The Barras (High Street). Whether you are looking for bargains or just listening to the sales patter, it is an experience not to be missed.

The Glasgow School of Art in Renfrew Street (Charing Cross) is a Charles Rennie Mackintosh building from the turn of the century.

Other places to visit include the Mitchell Library (Charing Cross) founded in 1874, the Kelvin Hall (which houses the Transport Museum) and Art Galleries (Patrick), the Botanic Gardens (Hillhead Underground), and the new Exhibition Centre (it has its own station, connected by a covered walkway, called Exhibition Centre!).

Pollok House (Pollokshaws West)
Built by William Adam in 1752, it has among its treasures a collection of Spanish art.

The 400-year-old Haggs Castle caters for children, with its 'activity methods' of learning about the past.

Arguably Scotland's top indoor attraction is the Burrell Collection (Pollokshaws West), beautifully displayed in its modern gallery, and popular with Glaswegians and visitors alike.

The televising of the annual Glasgow Marathon has shown the beauty of its architecture.

But perhaps Glasgow's fame is due to its friendly citizens who display helpfulness and humour in their dealings. Glasgow's motto 'Let Glasgow Flourish' has been modernised in the slogan 'Glasgow's Miles Better'.

GLASGOW SUBURBAN NETWORK
by Brian Forbes

Glasgow is the only Scottish city to retain a large suburban rail network with frequent electric trains along both banks of the Clyde; up to Balloch on the shores of Loch Lomond and out to Milngavie, Airdrie, Lanark, and Neilston. There are also diesel trains to the New Towns of Cumbernauld and East Kilbride; while in the city centre a self-contained Underground, with an unusual 4-foot gauge, describes a circle and serves fifteen stations – giving interchange with the surface lines at Patrick and Queen Street.

The electric services are operated in two sections; the north and east working out of Hyndland depot, and the south and south-west with units based at Shields Road depot. The Hyndland sets work six services, Airdrie to Helensburgh and Balloch using the 100-year-old tunnel under the city built by the Glasgow City & District Railway in 1886 but operated originally by the North British. Conversion to electric propulsion came in October 1960 with arguably still the best-looking electric multiple-units ever built. There is also a service between Springburn and Milngavie.

In April 1979, the disused tunnel under the 'Miles Better' city's famous Argyle Street shopping centre was reopened after fifteen years of decay, and named the 'Argyle line'. This united the previously separate northern and southern divisions of operation and a new station was built under Argyle Street. Some of the old stations were rebuilt on this former Lanarkshire & Dumbartonshire Railway – Stobcross, Finnieston, Central, Bridgeton Cross, and Dalmarnock. A new Rutherglen island platform was situated on this reopened route, with the previous four-platform station on the main line being made redundant. There was outcry at the time that the old stations of Glasgow Cross and Glasgow Green were not included, so much so that seven years later they are likely to come in the next stage of development.

This Argyle line is more usually referred to as 'Clyderail', and the Hamilton Circle and Lanark services have been diverted over it to Dalmuir. The last service north of the river is that of local relief trains between Dalmuir and High Street. All six services call at only two common stations, Partick and Hyndland, the latter giving easier interchange because of its island platform.

The South-side electrics were introduced in summer 1961, comprising the Cathcart Circle with its two offshoots, the Neilston and Newton branches. The Neilston was recently under threat of curtailment so as to electrify the East Kilbride branch, but there was much local opposition, plus a concerted effort by people to use the service, so these plans were dropped. The service to Newton connects there with Clyderail trains, giving people from the north a feeder into the south-side network. This line is, as you could imagine, very busy when major football matches are played at Hampden Park.

Most of the electric multiple-units are now painted in the colours of the benefactors, Strathclyde Passenger Transport Executive – orange bodies with black window surrounds. The original 1960 sets still operate successfully, although seven were withdrawn early on, owing to either accident or fire, and twelve have been sent south to Manchester. Out of the original ninety, fifty of the remainder have been refurbished, half a dozen with corridors between vehicles to facilitate onboard ticket examination. In 1967 further uprated, but similar-looking, sets came on stream, the 311s, but two of these have been cannibalised by Shields Road to enable the remainder to operate.

Strathcylde's suburban network is in a very healthy financial state – so much so that recently the Chairman of the Passenger Transport Executive held a meeting with groups wishing to extend the scope of the network. He, Malcolm Waugh, said he was convinced that certain routes which have been closed to passenger traffic for about twenty years were under consideration within the next stage of development. The PTE were looking at about a dozen possible station sites on the Shields Junction – High Street East Junction and Rutherglen – Coatbridge routes. Other stations were also being considered on the existing network because of a shift in population and industry. Asked if he would consider the reopening of certain dismantled sections, he vowed to look actively into any viable propositions.

Twenty-nine or thirty stations on dismantled or freight-only routes would be extremely popular additions. With the extra new stations proposed on existing or extended services as far as Grangemouth, the total is approaching fifty. Apart from the initial cost of electrification, which would probably be funded partly under the EEC, partly by local authority and the Government, the running cost is approximately 5p per mile. This compares with diesel multiple-units costs of about 27p per mile. The speedier, cleaner, and quieter electric services will be more appreciated by the public. Six months ago, before electrification of the Ayrline, there were eight bus companies running between Glasgow and the Ayrshire coast; now there are only two, and they are feeling the draught!

GLASGOW–GOUROCK/WEMYSS BAY
by John Tennant

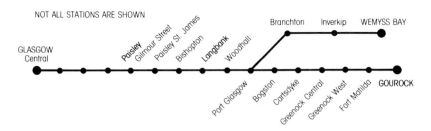

The lines from Glasgow to Gourock and Wemyss Bay are packed with interest for the visitor, whether he or she is keen on local history or simply enjoys a day out looking at beautiful scenery.

In former years, thousands of Glaswegians would go 'doon the watter' at holiday times, either sailing all the way from Glasgow or travelling by train to Gourock or Wemyss Bay and across on the railway-operated steamers to resorts such as Dunoon and Rothesay. Though one cannot make the whole journey by boat today – except on excursions on the *Waverley* – many still make the trip by train and boat.

The lines were electrified in 1967 and have been operated ever since by part of Glasgow's fleet of three-coach electric trains. These are known locally as the 'Blue trains' because when they were introduced all other passenger trains were green. The name is a misnomer nowadays, however, since the trains are now painted orange and black.

Progressive refurbishment of the rolling-stock has meant the loss to passengers of a forward view through the driver's compartment – a loss much regretted by small boys – and bigger ones, too! A smaller guard's compartment has resulted, but bicycles are still carried free of charge at the time of writing.

Journey times from Glasgow are about fifty minutes to Gourock and fifty-five minutes to Wemyss Bay. The Wemyss Bay service is hourly, stopping at all stations, while there are three trains an hour to Gourock, some of which do not stop at all stations.

Our journey begins at Glasgow's Central Station, usually at one of the higher-numbered platforms. Pulling out of the station, we immediately cross the River Clyde, with a good view of the city's skyline. On the right is the Kingston Bridge, carrying the M8 motorway over the river, while about the same distance away on the left is the bridge which once carried trains into St Enoch Station and, if an RDS reopening campaign succeeds, may one day allow trains from Glasgow's South electric lines to join the Queen Street Low Level line.

Presently we see on the left the tower blocks of the Gorbals, but these are soon hidden from view as we swing to the right and pass one of Glasgow's rail freight depots. The train now rapidly gathers speed, and before long we can see the Shields electric traction depot on the left. Many of Glasgow's suburban electric trains are maintained here, as are some main-line locomotives. At this point the train passes over the junction for the former Paisley Central line, closed against fierce opposition in January 1983. The track of this line diverges to the left – it is electrified as far as Corkerhill to provide access to the Corkerhill depot where the new Ayr line trains are maintained.

The M8 motorway now appears on the right and remains a close companion for the next couple of miles until we reach Cardonald Station. We are passing through the Ibrox area of Glasgow, famous for Rangers' football ground.

Just beyond Cardonald Station, a freight line diverges on the right to serve the King George V Dock, Barehead power-station, and part of the Hillington industrial estate. Indeed, very soon we pass this estate on the right, one of the first of its kind in the country, with factories belonging to such famous names as Rolls-Royce. The twin stations of Hillington East and Hillington West serve the estate and the residential area to the left of the line.

Shortly after we emerge into open countryside – but our spell in the country is brief, for little over ½ mile later we emerge from a cutting to see the skyline of Paisley. Some of the town's many spires and towers may be glimpsed from the train. Those interested in railways may look out for the trackbed of the former line to Renfrew, diverging on the right. On the left we may briefly see Paisley Abbey and the adjacent Town Hall before the train enters Gilmour Street Station.

It is well worth breaking your journey to explore Paisley. It has been a weaving centre from the year 1765 and possibly earlier, and the Paisley pattern and Paisley shawls are world famous. A collection of these shawls can be found at the Paisley Museum and Art Galleries, which also describes the history of the pattern as well as going into many aspects of local and natural history. Close to the Museum is the Coats Observatory, also open to the public. This was established in 1883 by the Paisley Philosophical Institution and financed by Mr Thomas Coats of the famous Paisley thread-making family. A factory bearing the name Coats still exists opposite the Shield electric traction depot mentioned earlier. The observatory's equipment includes a ten-inch Equatorial telescope built by Sir Howard Grubb in 1898.

Paisley is also famous for its Abbey, part of which dates from the twelfth century. We may reach it by walking 150 yards up Gilmour Street from the station to Paisley Cross and then turning left along Gauze Street. It contains one of the finest organs in Europe. Opposite the Abbey is the magnificent Town Hall with a Tourist Information Centre open all year (telephone 041–889 0711).

About 2½ miles north of Paisley lies Glasgow Airport, and there is a well-supplied taxi rank outside Gilmour Street Station for sightseers or intending air passengers.

Resuming our journey by train, we see the Ayr line going off to the left and behind it the Coats Observatory. We pass on a viaduct through an area of factories in various states of repair and presently arrive at Paisley St James Station after which we gather speed for the 4 mile scenic run to Bishopton. We pass under a road bridge to re-emerge in open countryside, soon joined on the right by the M8. Glasgow Airport can be seen on the right across the motorway, and in the distance the Kilpatrick Hills and the Campsie Fells. On the left are flat green fields with the Renfrew Heights beyond. Presently the motorway curves away to the right and the train enters woodland, which soon gives way to rolling fields on the right just before we enter Bishopton Station.

Bishopton is quite a large village and has long been the location of a Royal Ordnance factory, sidings for which can be seen to the left just beyond the station. From here one can cycle to the village of Erskine and perhaps across the Erskine Bridge to Old Kilpatrick from where it is possible to board trains on the North Clyde electric line.

We now pass through two short tunnels and come out on the south bank of the Clyde, with a magnificent view of the river. Dumbarton Rock is prominent on the north side with Dumbarton Castle built upon it. The River Leven, flowing from Loch Lomond, enters the Clyde at this point. Dumbarton has a long history of being a stronghold – the very name comes from the Gaelic for 'Fort of the Britons'.

Looking at the river itself, we see that it is very shallow and wide, the only navigable part being a channel marked by buoys, which needs continual dredging. As its name implies, Port Glasgow developed initially as Glasgow's port, but the provision of the channel enabled steamships to travel up to the city, forcing Port Glasgow to turn to shipbuilding.

Soon, unless we are on a fast train, we pause at the village of Langbank. Not far from here is the Finlaystone estate, with its outdoor recreational activities and its seasonal attraction of a doll and Victorian exhibitions. It may be reached by a walk or cycle ride of about 1¼ miles westwards along the coast road.

We then hasten on, at times coming very close to the water's edge, towards the unhappily declining heavy industry and shipbuilding of Port Glasgow and Greenock. After perhaps pausing briefly at Woodhall, an eastern residential suburb of Port Glasgow, we reach the town's station. Well worth a visit here are the ruins of Newark Castle, built in the sixteenth century by the Maxwells, and the full-size replica of Henry Bell's *Comet*, both near the shore road. The *Comet*, a passenger steamship designed by Henry Bell of Helensburgh, plied on the Clyde between Glasgow and Greenock from 1812 until it unfortunately sank in 1820.

Returning to the station, where drinks and light snacks may be bought, we notice the hand-painted armorial shields which decorate its walls. These are the work of Charles Wilson, a Senior Railman at Port Glasgow.

Port Glasgow–Gourock

The Gourock-bound train travels along a viaduct which gives fine views of Scott Lithgow's shipyard with its towering crane. Presently the Wemyss Bay line branches off to the left, and we have a brief glimpse of the harbour from which mainly tugs and fire-tenders operate. We call briefly at Bogston and Cartsdyke stations before arriving at Greenock Central.

Greenock was the birthplace of James Watt, the discoverer of steam-power, and was once a prosperous town as a result of trading with the Americas. The large modern container terminal at Prices Pier continues this tradition, though on a much smaller scale. This container terminal is served by a spur from the Wemyss Bay line and in former days there was also a passenger station here, handling boat trains for the emigrant ships anchored at the Tail of the Bank. Many troop trains also used Prices Pier in time of war.

Among Greenock's places of interest are the McLean Museum and Art Galleries, containing many Watt relics, and the building housing his scientific library. For details, contact the Information Centre in Cathcart Square, a few hundred yards from Central Station (telephone 0475–24400).

If we stay on the train, we immediately enter a tunnel, emerging about two minutes later at Greenock West Station. Another tunnel follows, and we soon arrive at Fort Matilda, which takes its name from an army barracks here during both world wars. Above the station, after a steep climb up Lyle Hill, stands the Cross of Lorraine, overlooking the Firth. This is a memorial to the Free French sailors who died in the Battle of the Atlantic in the Second World War.

The train continues the last mile or so downhill into Gourock, passing Cardwell Bay on the right where many yachts are moored, before entering the three-platform station beside Gourock Pier. The pier has recently been modernised and reduced in size, and handles Caledonian MacBrayne's ro-ro car ferry to Dunoon and their small passenger ferry to Kilcreggan. These ferries connect with the trains and through-ticketing is available. At the time of writing, the Dunoon ferry was hourly (including Sundays) and there were some six sailings a day to Kilcreggan (not Sundays). There is a taxi rank outside the station, and also bus shelters from which buses may be taken to places farther down the coast such as Wemyss Bay and Largs. (At the time of writing,

The M.V. *Jupiter* approaches Gourock from Dunoon, with the entrance to Loch Long behind her bridge. (*Photo:* John Tennant)

Clydeside Scottish provided an hourly service – telephone 0475–41388.

The scene from Gourock Pier on a fine day is among the best in Scotland, with views of the Holy Loch, Loch Long, and the Gareloch, and the Cowal Hills above Dunoon. There are also two submarine bases near by – the American base at the Holy Loch and the British one at Coulport on Loch Long. Gourock has long been familiar with naval vessels, however. During the Second World War, a boom was stretched from the Clock Lighthouse – just south of the town – across to Dunoon, which rendered the broad area known as the 'Tail of the Bank' a protected anchorage, where hundreds of ships of all types anchored and convoys were assembled.

Today's ferries take twenty minutes to cross to Dunoon, a popular holiday resort and the 'Gateway to the Cowal Peninsula', famous for its Castle Gardens and for the Younger Botanic Gardens a short bus trip away.

Port Glasgow to Wemyss Bay

If we board the Wemyss Bay train from Glasgow, it leaves the Gourock line soon after Port Glasgow Station and immediately begins to ascend into the hills, its electric power making easy work of the gradient. Fine views may now be enjoyed of Greenock, and across the water to Craigendoran, Helensburgh, and the Gareloch.

As the train continues its climb, now on single track, we see a spur diverging to the right and leading to the container terminal at Princes Pier. A little later on the left of the line we can glimpse the trackbed of the former line to Kilmacolm, which also went to Princes Pier. We then enter a short tunnel, and emerge to see on the right the Princes Pier spur crossing on a viaduct. The landscape is still urban, and soon we pass on the right the famous – and aromatic – Tate and Lyle sugar refinery, its rail connections unfortunately looking neglected.

Our next stop is Branchton, a new station opened in 1967 to serve quite a large residential area. The train then rumbles along the side of a wooded glen to IBM Halt, a new station serving exclusively the large IBM factory to the right of and below the line. Notice the mirrors and closed-circuit TV equipment on the platform here. This is to help the driver to see what is happening along the side of the train when he is operating the doors from his cab.

From IBM Halt, the train continues through wooded country, soon giving us a brief glimpse of the Firth of Clyde again on the right. Presently we encounter a passing loop just before Inverkip Station. This line used to have much more double track, as can be deduced from the occasional pillars which supported bridges for a second track.

The station building at Inverkip is nicely preserved, and nestles above the village, which is notable for its large marina – one of the largest in the country and still expanding. Another prominent landmark, which we see as we emerge from a short tunnel, is the Inverkip oil-fired power-station, with its towering, and allegedly cracked chimney. There are excellent views across the river to Dunoon and Innellan on the Cowal shore. We then drop into a cutting, at the end of which comes a splendid view of Bute, Toward Point and its lighthouse, and the entrance to the Kyles of Bute. Our train is now right beside the sea and entering Wemyss Bay's picturesque station, the end of the line.

This small station is one of the most attractive in Scotland. From its canopied platforms one can walk into a beautiful semicircular glass roofed concourse and down a broad covered ramp on to the pier itself, to board a Caledonian MacBrayne ferry to Rothesay on the Isle of Bute, half an hour away. Rothesay is a charming town, ranged round its bay, and has for many years been a popular holiday resort. Again, ferries

Passengers from Rothesay walk up from the ferry into Wemyss Bay station. (*Photo:* John Tennant)

connect with trains and there is through-ticketing. (At the time of writing, there are seven or eight sailings a day, but fewer on winter Sundays – for details telephone Gourock 33755). The station also has an elegant clock tower, a cafeteria and bar, and there is a bus shelter outside for local services along the A78 to places such as Gourock and Largs.

GLASGOW–AYR–GIRVAN–STRANRAER
by Graham Lund and Brian Chaplin

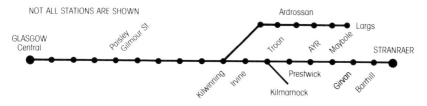

This line is heavily used by both commuters and tourists. Its fortunes received a welcome fillip in September 1986 when it was electrified as far as Ayr. Fast, comfortable, modern electric trains have now replaced ageing diesel multiple-units, operating at approximately half-hourly intervals. Services to Girvan run approximately 2 hourly during the daytime, and Stranraer is served by about six trains a day, two of which run via Kilmarnock to Carlisle and London, catering for travellers using the ferries that ply between Stranraer and Larne in Northern Ireland.

Immediately after departing from Glasgow Central Station our train crosses the

The opening ceremony of the Ayrshire electrification. The moment was 'electrifying' when the cord to break the champagne bottle over the train broke in Councillor Waugh's hand! (*Photo: The Glasgow Herald*)

An electrification construction team erecting masts on the £84 million Ayrline project. (*Photo:* British Rail)

Clyde, and for the next few miles the scene is predominantly industrial, with many large factories – including Rolls-Royce's plant at Hillington – located near the railway.

Paisley, a busy industrial town with a population of about 100,000, is our next stop. It is perhaps best known for its Abbey and for the fine shawls with their distinctive patterns woven here during the early nineteenth century. Now it is the largest thread-producing town in the world, and the home of Robertson's Jam factory. In railway terms it forms the junction of the lines to Ayr and Stranraer, and to Gourock and Wemyss Bay.

Johnstone Station constitutes part of an 'Interlink' scheme whereby buses deliver passengers at the station car park to continue their journeys by rail.

Our train now skirts along the shores of Black Cart Water and Castle Semple Loch before halting at Lockwinnoch, which is set amid pleasant moorland near the Ayrshire–Renfrewshire border. Then, after passing Loch Kilbirnie, we stop at Glengarnock, a former steel town. For the next few miles the line runs parallel with the River Garnock. Just north of Dalry, which manufactures furniture on a small scale, we pass the Roche pharmaceutical factory, which is rail-connected.

Kilwinning, our next stop and the junction of the branch to Ardrossan and Largs, is reputed to be the earliest home in Scotland of Freemasonry, probably introduced by foreign workers who came to build the Abbey here in the twelfth century.

Irvine, lying at the confluence of the rivers Garnock and Irvine, may be described as a modern industrial town with an ancient past. Although it is one of Scotland's oldest burghs, it ranks as one of the five New Towns designed to alleviate Glasgow's housing problems, and has grown immensely in recent years as a result. Its industry includes a large chemical complex.

Continuing southward, we pass the first of a series of golf-courses for which

68

Ayrshire is famed. Just before Barassie Station the charmingly named Stinking Rocks may be seen offshore. The next stop is Troon, which has a harbour with a number of yacht berths and a shipbuilding and shipbreaking yard. But the resort is best known for its excellent golf-courses and was the venue for the British Open Golf Championship in 1981.

At Prestwick there are further views of the coast and golf-courses. The international airport, whose fog-free record contributed to its rapid growth during the Second World War when it became the headquarters of RAF Ferry Command and of the USAF Air Transport Command, since when it has reverted to a civil airport and has recently been designated a freeport. A few buses operate from the station to the airport, although only a dual carriageway separates it from the disused station at Monkton whose fabric remains still intact.

Near Newton-on-Ayr there is a freight line to Ayr docks used by merry-go-round trains carrying coal destined for Kilroot power-station in Ireland. And immediately south of the locomotive depot is the junction of the former line to Mauchline, still lying largely intact and used by the occasional train to Killoch Colliery. Crossing the River Ayr, we obtain fleeting glimpses of the town's various bridges.

Ayr's newly refurbished station befits the historic town, which owes at least something of its prosperity to its ties with Robert Burns. Outside the station stands a statue of the poet; and in High Street is the little Tam o' Shanter Inn, now a museum, which was possibly the starting-point of Tam's adventurous ride to Alloway on his 'grey meare Meg'. From the new bridge, by which the main road crosses the river, is a good view of the thirteenth-century 'Auld Brig' that figures in the poem 'The Brigs of Ayr'. Two miles south of the town lies Alloway, the village were Burns was born in 1759 and lived his first seven years. Adjoining Burns' Cottage is a museum containing an important collection of manuscripts, letters, and other relics of the poet.

Ayr is also one of Scotland's most popular holiday resorts, with its sandy beaches, its racecourse (venue of the Scottish Grand National), and Butlin's holiday camp.

About 8 miles south is the imposing eighteenth-century Culzean Castle, until 1945 the seat of the Kennedys of Dunure and now owned by the National Trust for Scotland.

Train services south of Ayr are all diesel-operated. The single track twists and turns through beautiful undulating countryside towards the Carrick Hills. Maybole, our next stop, is a sleepy town with a reputation for making footwear and agricultural implements. Buses run from the town to Turnberry golf-course when the Open Championship is held there. A few miles out lies the ruined but impressive Crossraguel Abbey.

Girvan, a coastal resort of some 8,000 inhabitants, boasts a harbour, a spacious waterfront, sandy beaches, and offers good freshwater and seafishing. From here can be seen Ailsa Craig, a 1,114-foot-high granite rock lying 10 miles offshore; it is part bird sanctuary and part quarry supplying a special granite used to make the best curling stones.

Leaving Girvan, we obtain some fine retrospective views of the town and Ailsa Craig. On our right can be discerned Byne Hill with its jagged top. As we ascend the Carrick Hills in the company of the A714 road to Newton Stewart we pass through pleasant wooded valleys.

At this point our route turns inland; the coast south of Girvan is accessible only by road. The A77 road to Ballantrae is particularly attractive, and Kennedy's Pass dramatically so. Formerly a notorious haunt of smugglers, Ballantrae is now a fishing port, as well as a centre for forestry and agriculture – notably Ayrshire early potatoes.

After emerging from Pinmore Tunnel, which is 469 metres long, we pass the hamlet of Pinmore with its tiny school near the line; and about 1½ miles beyond Pinmore Viaduct we may observe the River Stinchar flowing from the east. Speeds on this section of line are not high owing to the tightness of its curves and the severity of its gradients.

At Pinwherry, the first of four passing places, the River Stinchar joins the River Duisk, which eventually flows into the sea at Ballantrae; this we follow all the way to Barrhill, Strathclyde's most southerly station.

Just before arriving at Barrhill, we may see on the left Kildonan Convent surrounded by wooded gardens and situated beside the A714. Inside the entrance hall of Barrhill's tidy station is a particularly fine Caledonian Railway Company clock. Although the station is 1½ miles from the village, it serves as a useful railhead from which to tour the surrounding countryside, be it on foot or by bicycle.

We leave Barrhill and climb to Chirmorie summit, the highest point on the route, passing through afforested moorland. The summit may be easily identified by a small mast that stands on top of the hill at Chirmorie. We now enter Dumfries and Galloway – one of Scotland's loveliest yet least-known regions. Here our train begins the descent to the coast, passing Arecleoch Forest on the right. The weather can be wild on this desolate plateau, especially in winter; and on the left from time to time can be seen fencing – albeit in poor order – to protect the line from snowdrifts. The river we cross several times is the Cross Water of Luce, which flows southward to Luce Bay.

From Glenwhilly, where tokens are exchanged as our train enters a passing loop,

Ayr. (*Photo:* E. West)

we descend sharply the 1:57 gradient to New Luce. Here, on its course south, the Cross Water of Luce joins the Main Water of Luce. On the left we may catch a glimpse of the hamlet of New Luce, with its football pitch, park, and boarded-up station building.

Our journey continues along the ever-widening valley. On the left we pass Glenluce Abbey, which was founded in 1192 as a Cistercian house by Roland, Earl of Galloway; although now ruined, it contains some noteworthy architectural features. The tall castellated mansion also visible on the left is the Castle of Park; it was built by Thomas Hay, son of the last Abbot of Glenluce, using stones from the abbey.

As the line begins to turn westward, the trackbed of the abandoned Dumfries–Stranraer line – the so called 'Paddy route' – comes into sight from the east; and, at about the same time, to the south and west there are clear views of Luce Bay and the Rhins Peninsula whose southernmost extremity, the Mull of Galloway, is marked by 200-foot-high cliffs and a lighthouse.

At Dunragit we enter the last passing loop before Stranraer. The factory with a tall chimney next to the line produces soups and belongs to Nestlé. On the left we pass in turn Torrs Warren, an area characterised by sand-dunes and forestry, and the disused buildings of Castle Kennedy Station. Finally, before entering the environs of Stranraer, we may observe Sheuchan Hill and Loch Ryan, which is 8 miles long and nearly 3 miles wide, and at whose head lies Stranraer.

Alongside Stranraer's newly modernized harbour station are moored the ferries that make the two-hour trip to the Irish coast at Larne, some 30 miles away. In summer day-trip tickets to Ireland are available from Sealink's office.

Stranraer itself, with a population of about 11,000, is the second largest town in Dumfries and Galloway. Besides being an important commercial centre, it is a lively holiday resort, containing numerous hotels and guest-houses. From the parapet walkway of its ruined sixteenth-century castle there are good views of the town and the surrounding area.

Stranraer makes an excellent base from which to explore the west of Galloway. Buses run to Drummore, near the Mull of Galloway Lighthouse; to Logan Botanic Gardens, which contain many subtropical plants and shrubs which thrive there owing to the mild influence of the Gulf Stream; to Newton Stewart and thence to Whithorn, which is closely connected with St Ninian who first brought Christianity to Scotland in about the year 400. Easily reached along the A75 are the gardens at Lochinch Castle (Castle Kennedy), the stately Scots-French mansion of the Earl of Stair. The gardens are famous for their rhododendrons and for their monkey puzzle trees, many of which are over a hundred years old and 70 feet high. Lastly, it is possible to enjoy a scenic ride to Dumfries using service buses – the nearest we can get to travelling the old 'Paddy route' whose unfortunate closure in the Beeching era not only greatly extended journey times of services between Stranraer and Carlisle (that were re-routed via Kilmarnock and Ayr) but cut off a large region from the rail network.

KILWINNING–LARGS
by Graham Lund

An hourly service operates between Glasgow and Largs with additional trains during peak times. From Kilwinning, where it parts company with the line to Ayr and Stranraer, our newly electrified line branches westward before proceeding northward through a succession of coastal towns. Its rural aspect is soon lost as we approach ICI's huge factory at Stevenson, our first stop.

A mile and a quarter farther on we come to Saltcoats, a bustling holiday resort popular with many Glaswegians. The town owes its name to the saltworks established here by James V.

Adjoining Saltcoats is Ardrossan, another popular resort, whose importance is as a port for sailings to Arran and the Isle of Man. In summer a few passenger trains run along the 1¼-mile long spur linking Ardrossan harbour.

Leaving Ardrossan, our train heads towards Seamill and West Kilbride, which has a late fifteenth-century castle. We then lose sight of the coast temporarily before reaching the British Steel Corporation's giant deep-water iron-ore terminal at Hunterston, which was completed in 1979 at the cost of £98,000,000. Once the ore has been offloaded from the ore-carriers docked here, it is transported by rail.

Our train halts next at Fairlie, a pleasant resort with a sixteenth-century castle perched at the top of a pretty glen above the town. We continue on the last three miles of our journey; and, after emerging from a long tunnel, see unfolding before us a glorious panorama of the Clyde coast and the island of the Great Cumbrae. The only town on the Great Cumbrae is Millport situated at the southern end of the island; it can easily be reached by steamer from Largs.

Largs itself has a population of 9,800 and, lying in a sheltered position below lofty green hills, is a very popular seaside resort with good bathing beaches. From its Douglas Park, which ascends to 600 feet, there are magnificent views of the sea, islands, and mountains.

KILMARNOCK–AYR
by Graham Lund

This 8 mile line is not distinguished for its scenic qualities, passing as it does through two disused stations – at Gatehead and Drybridge – and the former Massey Ferguson tractor plant, now an industrial estate. Its importance lies in its strategic role as a link between Kilmarnock on the Nith Valley route and Barassie on the Glasgow–Stranraer route, a role reinforced since the 1960s with the re-routing of the London–Stranraer service following the closure of the direct line between Dumfries and Stranraer. However, its potential remains unrealised; for, with the exception of the twice-daily London–Stranraer service and a summer-only Kilmarnock–Ayr diesel multiple-unit service, it is used by no scheduled passenger trains. However it would be possible now to divert via Kilmarnock some Glasgow–Stranraer trains, taking advantage of the greater operational flexibility of the new Sprinters.

GLASGOW–KILMARNOCK–DUMFRIES–CARLISLE
by Graham Lund and Brian Chaplin

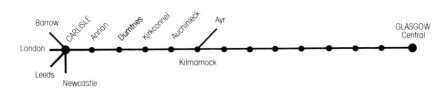

There is a half-hourly local service on the first section of this route as far as Barrhead, with alternate trains running through to Kilmarnock. Services south of Kilmarnock, however, operate less frequently, with gaps of two hours or more between them.

After departing from Glasgow Central Station, our train crosses the Clyde, of which there are panoramic views from both sides of the carriage. Passengers may not realise that the Gorbals, which have recently been redeveloped, lie directly south of the river, near Bridge Street Underground station. Two miles farther, we pass the City Transport Museum on the left, though this line provides no direct access.

The built-up area as far as Barrhead is served by Crossmyloof, Pollokshaws West (where the East Kilbride branch diverges), Kennishead, and Nitshill.

Leaving Barrhead, our train climbs steeply and the scene rapidly changes from an urban to a rural one; we are now on a single track for most of the 16¾ miles to Kilmarnock. A notable feature to the west is Loch Libo, whose waters flow within feet of our train. We enter a passing loop at Uplawmoor, where a freight-only line runs to Beith.

Dunlop is the first of three single-platform stations, situated in pleasant countryside; as other forms of public transport are scarce, its rail service is a lifeline. Still in good agricultural country, Stewarton, an expanding town, also relies heavily on its trains. Local clothing-manufacturers cannot absorb all the available labour, so many workers have to commute to Glasgow each day. The large viaduct south of the station crosses the Irvine and Kilmarnock road and Annick Water. Kilmaurs, another growing town, had its station rebuilt in May 1984, which, though poorly sited, is used by many commuters.

Kilmarnock, home of Burns's first edition of poetry, hosts Johnnie Walker's Whisky bottling plant – the world's biggest – which is adjacent to the station, where the branch to Barassie and Ayr diverges. The town, which is also an important agricultural centre, manufactures carpets and light engineering products. Here the firm of Andrew Barclay recently assembled a batch of Class 143 railbuses for use on the Tyne and Wear Metro.

Leaving Kilmarnock, we cross a twenty-three-arch viaduct from which on the left can be seen a disused Victorian hospital and on the right an excellent view of the town. Once across Kilmarnock Water we pass Kay Park and Burns's Monument, where many of the poet's original works are housed. The former Riccarton loop, now truncated, forms a spur to the right, just on the edge of the town, and still carries oil traffic. About 2 miles farther we cross a seven-arch bridge over the River Irvine, before passing Barrleith, Johnnie Walker's warehouse being next to the former line to Darvel. A further 8 miles on, just south of Mauchline Junction, lies Ballochmyle Viaduct spanning a narrow, deep-wooded ravine where the River Ayr flows rapidly towards the coast; this is claimed to be the highest single-span masonry viaduct in the world.

Auchinleck's station reopened in May 1984 after eight years' work by the District and Regional Councillors, and the Railway Development Society. It is located close to the town centre and new housing. Look west to catch a glimpse of the towers above Killoch Pit and east to see the trackbed of the disused line to Muirkirk.

After passing Cumnock, Creoch Loch, and Loch o' the Lowes, we enter New Cumnock – a prime candidate for a new station – and meet the River Nith where it is joined by Burns's immortal Afton Water. Any coal trains we pass on this section of line are likely to have originated from the new coalfields of South Ayrshire; other freight trains may well convey goods destined for Northern Ireland via Ayr, and pet foods for Cambridgeshire. Sadly, co-ordination between buses and trains here remains poor, with thorough-ticketing virtually non-existent.

We are now near the source of the River Nith, which we shall follow closely as far as

Dumfries, about 35 miles away. The importance of the river is reflected in the name commonly used for this line – 'The Nith Valley Route'. Kirkconnel, situated on the northern fringe of the Dumfries and Galloway Region, is a small mining town, at whose station those wishing to explore Upper Nithsdale on foot or by bicycle should alight. The wild upland scenery of the district is well worth exploring; and it is from here that easy access can be gained to The Southern Upland Way Long Distance Walk – 212 miles from Portpatrick in the west to Cockburnspath in the east. The neighbouring town of Sanquhar also merits a visit, a Royal Burgh since 1484, and possessing a ruined sixteenth-century castle, a tolbooth dated 1735, and the oldest post office in the United Kingdom. Unemployment in the area remains high because of the contraction of the mining industry in recent years – most miners are now taken by bus to the Killoch and Barony pits in South Ayrshire. However, new coalfields are being developed, and British Rail should secure the lion's share of any transport contracts. Finally, the exemplary smartness of Kirkconnel's recently modernised station for which the Regional Council gave financial assistance demonstrates how such co-operation between BR and local authorities can be mutually beneficial.

Heading south, we enter the most attractive but little-known Drumlanrig Gorge through which flows the swirling River Nith. The railway and road here being perched on the eastern side of the gorge. Views of the forested valley sides are suddenly interrupted when our train goes through Drumlanrig Tunnel, after which it passes the village of Carronbridge, some 3 miles north of the market town of Thornhill.

Thornhill is a charming little town with a population of 1,500, situated in the heart of Mid Nithsdale. It has a long association with the Dukes of Buccleuch and Queensberry, whose home is Drumlanrig Castle some 3½ miles north of the town. The castle, which is visible from the train after Carronbridge, was built between 1679 and 1690 for the first Duke of Queensberry, using local pink sandstone; it consists of four towers with seventeen lead turrets erected round a courtyard, and contains a remarkable collection of paintings – including works by Rembrandt, Holbein, Murillo, Reynolds, and Ramsay – and French furniture. Its grounds are extensive, offering miles of good walking beside lochs and burns and through forests and woods. What a shame, therefore, that Thornhill Station is closed! The old platforms and buildings still survive, the latter being used by British Rail as a permanent-way depot; a reopened station would undoubtedly benefit walkers and cyclists wishing to explore the area, as well as local people.

The valley now begins to broaden, though hills on either side are never out of sight. This is rich dairy-farming country and herds of Ayrshire cattle can often be seen when our train passes Closeburn, where the A76 road runs near the line. At Auldgirth look out for the elegant old sandstone road bridge over the Nith; it is now used only by pedestrians, having been replaced by one of functional design. We leave the road and continue downstream, crossing the river many times until the town of Dumfries comes into view

A perambulation round Dumfries is delightful. The wide river, handsome sandstone buildings, and five fine bridges, the oldest of which dates back to 1426, together make up an attractive scene. In 1986 Dumfries celebrated its 800th anniversary as a Royal Burgh by establishing the Burns' Heritage Trust in honour of the poet with whom it has a particularly strong association. Mercifully the town escaped the ravages of the tower-block planners of the 1960s and possesses several buildings of merit. These include Midsteeple in High Street; Crichton Royal Hospital; Burns's statue; and, on a hill across the river, the Borough Museum. This latter incorporates an eighteenth-century windmill, housing a camera obscura giving a coloured moving picture of the town.

Dumfries, the gateway to Galloway, makes an excellent centre from which to explore the many unspoilt villages along the Solway Firth that in the past were often frequented by smugglers. However, since the Beeching closure in the direct route to Stranraer, rail passengers wishing to reach destinations farther west have had to travel by bus. Most buses depart from a riverside area known as 'Whitesands'. Especially useful are Western Scottish Service 76 to Stranraer; and, for those interested in the smugglers' villages, Peacock's coach services to New Abbey, Kirkbean, Southwick, and Rockcliffe. Other places of interest within a 6-mile radius include Lincluden Abbey, a twelfth-century Benedictine convent; Sweetheart Abbey, a Cistercian foundation so called because Devorgilla Balliol, its founder, was buried there in 1273 together with her husband's heart that she had carried round with her for some sixteen years; Caerlaverock Castle, which dates from about 1290, and which, unusually, is triangular in form, with a moat still full of water; and Caerlaverock National Nature Reserve, which is noted for its winter wildfowl, particularly Barnacle geese, and for being the most northerly breeding ground of the Natterjack toad.

Between Dumfries and Annan the railway follows the edge of the Solway Firth. Presently we pass the village of Ruthwell, whose church contains a fine 18-foot-high cross dating from the seventh century, an important relic of Dark Ages Europe. The church may easily be reached by using Western Scottish Service 79 from Dumfries to Carlisle. Journeying east, we obtain glimpses of the Solway and the fells of the English Lake District in the distance on the right; and of the hills towards Lockerbie on the left.

After crossing the River Annan, we halt at the station of the town to which the river gives its name. Annan is a busy town of 8,000 inhabitants, closely connected with fishing and local farming. From here the scenery becomes less inspiring as we traverse the flat terrain adjoining the Solway. We pass the villages of Dornock, Eastriggs, and Rigg before Gretna Green, the traditional destination of countless runaway couples; on our left lies the disused station, on our right the A75 Euroroute to Stranraer and Northern Ireland. Here we take our leave of Dumfries and Galloway, one of Britain's lowest populated, least-known yet most scenic regions. Most visitors make their way to the Scottish Highlands; but those in search of peace and solitude amid superb scenery could do no better than make an excursion into Scotland's south-west.

We join the electrified West Coast Main Line at Gretna Junction, 9 miles north of Carlisle, and speed through the frequently fought-over Border territory towards Carlisle's Citadel Station and our journey's end, when we shall have travelled a total of 115½ miles.

WHAT IS THE RAILWAY DEVELOPMENT SOCIETY?

The Railway Development Society is a national, voluntary independent body which campaigns for better rail services, both for passenger and for freight, and greater use of rail transport.

It publishes books and papers, holds meetings and exhibitions, sometimes runs special trains and generally endeavours to put the case for rail to politicians, civil servants, commerce and industry, and the public at large, as well as feeding users' comments and suggestions to British Rail management and unions.

Membership is open to all who are in general agreement with the aims of the Society and subscriptions (as at June 1987) are:

Standard rate: £7.50

Students, pensioners, unemployed: £4

Families: £7 plus £1 for each member of household.

Special rates apply for corporate bodies.

Write to the Membership Secretary, Mr F. J. Hastilow, 21 Norfolk Road, Sutton Coldfield, West Midlands, B75 6SQ.

RDS SCOTLAND – ITS PLACE
by Hugh Neville (Hon. Secretary)

Post-war attempts to obtain for the railway system in Scotland the degree of public support which it merits fall roughly into four phases.

Until 1961/2 was the phase of general apathy. Resistance to the many withdrawals of passenger services was patchy and ineffective.

From 1961/2 till the early 1970s, the Scottish Railway Development Association, among other bodies (the best known being nicknamed 'MacPuff', which was backed by the late Professor E. R. Hondelink), put fairly continuous effort into opposing the programme of cuts presided over by the then British Railway's Chairman, Dr Beeching. The very limited measure of success was none the less very important: among lines saved were the West Highland and those to the north and west of Inverness.

From about 1972, much of Scotland now being denuded of its railways, the need to campaign for co-ordination of bus and train was paramount, and to advocate this the SRDA changed its name to 'Scottish Association for Public Transport'.

In 1982, however, the danger of another dose of anti-railwayism was becoming apparent, and a few members of the SAPT left to form an 'Ad Hoc Committee for the Defence of Railways'. This committee sparked off the idea of a petition against the Serpell Report (which had suggested further large-scale closures) and this idea was swiftly taken up by the RDS. The committee converted itself from being an 'ad hoc' body into being the Scottish branch of the RDS, and has since used the name RDS Scotland.

Incidentally, almost half of the 250,000 signatures to the petition, which was presented by the RDS at 10 Downing Street on 30 June 1983, came from Scotland.

The production of a railguide represents a rather different venture from what we have been doing for a quarter of a century. It was, however, the success of the railguides compiled by our colleagues in England and Wales which prompted suggestions for a Scottish counterpart. As it covers a considerably larger area than the other books in the series, we have not managed to describe every line in detail; but this may be remedied in a future edition. We hope that what we have provided has a value not too much impaired by what is missing.

This is not really the place to go into individual cases. SAPT easily survived the loss of the few who put their effort into the 'ad hoc' committee and then into RDS Scotland. I think it is doubtful whether, had not *both* SAPT *and* RDS Scotland existed to advocate the Dornoch Firth rail crossing, this project would ever have become a live political issue. Two bodies pulling together are better than one!

For further information about the RDS, write to the General Secretary, Trevor Garrod, 15 Clapham Road, Lowestoft, Suffolk, NR32 1RQ.

For further information about RDS Scotland, write to: Mr F. H. Neville, 351 Kingsway, Dundee.

RAIL-USER'S GROUPS

In addition to RDS Scotland, the following local groups concern themselves with campaigning for, and promoting, specific lines:

Glasgow–East Kilbride Railway Development Association. Secretary: Mrs Helen Broadbent, 92 Hillview Drive, Clarkston, Glasgow, G76 7JD. The association has fought for the retention and improvement of this line since the 1960s.

Cumbernauld Commuters' Association, Secretary: Andrew Stephen, 71 Cedar Road, Abronhill, Cumbernauld, G67 3AR. Founded in 1978, the association has achieved Inter-City status for Cumbernauld Station and is campaigning for a direct link to Glasgow.

Friends of the West Highland Line. Membership Secretary: Charles O'Neill, Flat 10/2, 39 Rosemount Street, Glasgow, G21 2JU. Formed in 1983, the society has branches in Oban, Glasgow, and London, conducts local market research and has many activities to promote the line, including a film for hire.

North Berwick Line Committee Secretary: Norman Renton, 23 Abbey Court, North Berwick, East Lothian, EH39 4BY. A local authority committee set up originally when the line was threatened with closure.

FURTHER INFORMATION

Scottish Tourist Board: 23 Ravelston Terrace, Edinburgh, EH4 3EU (Tel: 031-332–2433)

Maps
We recommend the Ordnance Survey maps, of various scales – for details write to Information and Public Enquiries, Ordnance Survey, Romsey Road, Maybush, Southampton, SO9 4DH. Also very useful are the National series published by John Bartholomew & Sons, Ltd, Duncan Street, Edinburgh, EH9 1TA.

Bibliography
Famedram Publishers Ltd, have published four books on individual lines by Tom Weir: *The Highland Line; The Mallaig Line; The Kyle Line; The Oban Line.* Other useful books are:
The Highland Railway by H. A. Vallance (David & Charles).
The West Highland Railway by John Thomas (David & Charles).
The Skye Railway by John Thomas (David & Charles).
The Railways of Fife by William Scott Bruce (Melven Press, Perth, 1980).
All Stations to Mallaig by John A. Mcgregor (Bradford Barton, 1982).

British Railway Journeys (King's Cross to the North) by Carolin Dakers (Fourth Estate, 1985).
Regional History of the Railways of Britain Vol. 6 – *Scotland* by John Thomas (David & Charles).
Forgotten Railways: Scotland (deals with closed lines) by John Thomas (David & Charles).

Rail Services

British Rail publishes a timetable covering the whole of Great Britain, running to over 1,400 pages, each May and September. It can be bought at staffed stations and many bookshops, or consulted in public libraries. In addition, a wide range of free timetable booklets and leaflets, for individual lines or groups of lines, are available, together with leaflets on special offers, sleeper services, bicycles by train, etc.

British Rail's Scottish Region now uses the name ScotRail. Principal station information offices are:

Aberdeen	Tel: 0224–594222	Inverness	Tel: 0463–238924
Dundee	Tel: 0382–28046	Perth	Tel: 0738–37117
Edinburgh	Tel: 031–556-2451	Stirling	Tel: 0786–64754
Glasgow	Tel: 041–204-2844		

Bus Services

Bus deregulation introduced under the 1986 Transport Act means that information about services can quickly become out of date. We cannot, therefore, accept any responsibility for such information – but the bus companies listed below were known to be operating in Scotland at the time of going to press:

Blue Band Motors, Bridge Street Garage, Lockerbie, Dumfries & Galloway (Tel: 2132/3/4).

Central Scottish Omnibuses, Traction House, Hamilton Road, Motherwell, ML1 3DS (Tel: 63575).

Clydeside Scottish Omnibuses, 5 Gordon Street, Paisley, PA1 1XE.

Eastern Scottish Omnibuses, New Street, Edinburgh, EH8 8DW (Tel: 031–556–2515).

Fife Scottish Omnibuses, Esplanade, Kirkcaldy, Fife, KY1 1SP (Tel: 261461/6).

Gibson, James & Sons, 16 Church Street, Moffat, Dumfries & Galloway (Tel: 20200).

Graham's Bus Services Ltd, Hawkhead Garage, Hawkhead Road, Paisley, PA2 7BA (Tel: 041–887–3831/2/3).

Grampian Regional Transport, King Street, Aberdeen, AB9 aSP (Tel: 637047).

Kelvin Scottish Omnibuses, Suite 2, 101 Westerhill Road, Bishopbriggs, Glasgow.

Highland Scottish Omnibuses, Seafield Road, Inverness, IV1 1TN (Tel: 237575).

Lothian Regional Transport, 14 Queen Street, Edinburgh, EH2 1JL (Tel: 031–554–4494).

Lowland Scottish Omnibuses, Duke Street, Galashiels, Borders, TD1 1QA.

Midland Scottish Omnibuses, Brown Street, Camelon, Falkirk, FK1 4PY (Tel: 23901/5).

Northern Scottish Omnibuses, Guild Street, Aberdeen, AB9 2DR (Tel: 51381).

T. Pateron & Brown Ltd, 51 Holmhead, Kilbirnie, Ayrshire, KA25 6BS (Tel: 3344).

Strathclyde Passenger Transport Authority, Consort House, West George Street, Glasgow, G2 1HN (Tel: 041–332–6811).

Strathtay Scottish Omnibuses, 5 Whitehall Crescent, Dundee, DD1 4AR.

Tayside Regional Council, Friarfield House, Barrack Street, Dundee, DD1 1PG (Tel: 23281).

M. Taylor, Westerbus, Badbea, Dundonnell, Wester Ross.

West Coast Motor Service Co, Saddell Street, Campbeltown, Argyllshire (Tel: 2319).
Western Scottish Omnibuses, Nursey Avenue, Kilmarnock, KA1 3JD (Tel: 22551/6).
E. Yule, Station Crossing Garage, Pitlochry, Perthshire (Tel: 2290).

Ferries

Services from Oban and Mallaig to the Western Isles and from Ardrossan to Arran are operated by Caledonian MacBrayne Ltd; for details contact them at Ferry Terminal, Gourock, PA19 1QP.

Services to the Orkney Islands (from Scrabster with bus connection from Thurso Station) and the Shetland Islands (from Aberdeen) are operated by P & O Ferries, PO Box No. 5, Aberdeen, AB9 8DL (Tel: 572615).

Steam Railways

Some of the preserved lines operating steam services are mentioned in the description of the nearest British Rail line. Here is a list of lines most likely to be of interest to the tourist, and where to obtain further details:

The Caledonian Railway (Brechin). Enquiries to Brechin Station, 2 Park Road, Brechin, Angus, DD9 7AF.

Bo'ness & Kinneil Railway. Enquiries to: Bo'ness Station, Union Street, Bo'ness, West Lothian, EH51 0AD (Tel: 0506–822298).

Strathspey Railway (Aviemore–Boat of Garten). Enquiries to Boat of Garten Station, Inverness-shire, PH24 3BH (Tel: 047983–692).

Kerr's Miniature Railway, West Links Park, Arbroath, Angus (Tel: 0241–79249).

Mull & West Highland Railway – Scotland's only passenger train on an island. Enquiries to Oban Tourist Information Office (Tel: 06803–389/472).

Lochty Private Railway, East Fife. Opened in 1967 as the first preserved steam passenger line in Scotland, accessible via the B940 Cupar–Crail road. Enquiries to Mr P. M. Westwater, FRPG Secretary, 48 Hendry Road, Kirkicaldy, Fife, KY2 5JN.

Other Books in the Series

All of the above are obtainable from the RDS Sales Officer, Geoff Kent, 21 Fleetwind Drive, East Hunsbury, Northampton, NN4 0ST, from the respective local branches, from bookshops, or from the publishers, Jarrold Colour Publications, Barrack Street, Norwich NR3 1TR.

INDEX

ISBN 0-7117-0299-3
© 1987 Railway Development Society
Printed and published in Great Britain by Jarrold and Sons Ltd, Norwich. 187